WRITING SOUTH CAROLINA

Seniors—*front row, left to right:* Aimee McVey, Milner Martin, Nicolas Fernandez, Amairany Aguirre, Brandi Cunningham, Alexis Etheredge, Jasmine Shabazz, Hannah Jane Pearson; *second row, left to right:* Mary Alice Monroe, Melis Tirhi, Abby Johanson, Kenni Ojediran, Megan Jensen, Isis McNeal, Taylor Widener, Sarah Williams-Shealy, Erintrude Wrona, Aïda Rogers; *third row, left to right:* Steven Lynn, Christian Eitel, Jared Mack, Katherine Kristinik, Tavashia Berry, Morgan Rizer, Mallory Clamp, Andrew Herbst, Maxwell T. Hall, Anna Sheppard.

Absent: Jamie Altman, Michelle Barton, John Sterling Poole

Photograph by Allen Anderson

Juniors—*bottom row, left to right:* Bailey Babb, Alexandra Hurd, Alyssa Conner, Candace Beebe, Breanna Murrin, Manogna Kolluru; *second row, left to right:* Mary Alice Monroe, Patsy Mejia-Rocha, Emily Brooke, Sarah Finleyson, Jaynae Jefferson, Morgan Blankenbecklor, Mya' Johnson-Jones; *third row, left to right:* Erin Hackney, Hali Hutchinson, Issac Blackwell, Hampton Slate, Alan Lanxton, Alaina Kiffer.

Absent: De-Jah Burton, Eliza Kapeluck, Sydny Long, Zyria Rodgers

Photograph by Allen Anderson

WRITING
SOUTH CAROLINA

VOLUME 3

Selections from the Third Annual
High School Writing Contest

Edited by Aïda Rogers and Steven Lynn
Foreword by Mary Alice Monroe

The University of South Carolina Press

© 2018 University of South Carolina

Published by the University of South Carolina Press
Columbia, South Carolina 29208

www.sc.edu/uscpress

Manufactured in the United States of America

27 26 25 24 23 22 21 20 19
10 9 8 7 6 5 4 3 2

Library of Congress Cataloging-in-Publication data
can be found at http://catalog.loc.gov/.

ISBN 978-1-61117-918-7 (paperback)
ISBN 978-1-61117-919-4 (ebook)

CONTENTS

Seniors

FOREWORD

Life is one long story. Birth and death. Happiness and sorrow. Rejection and acceptance. For a writer, all life's experiences are fodder for stories. I write today to celebrate the significant and important stories, essays, and poems written by the finalists of the third South Carolina High School Writing Contest, presented in this esteemed collection, *Writing South Carolina*.

I am in awe of the contributors in this book. They are astonishingly talented, further ahead in the game than I was at their age. I applaud them for this important achievement and validation. Each of them can now claim the honor of being a published writer.

It took me much longer to cross that line. I am one of ten children, the third eldest. My family is a well of material I've tapped into many times as a writer. Some of my happiest childhood memories are rooted in story. I was an avid reader, and when I was unhappy with an ending or wanted more, I wrote my own version. The art of creating stories lived in me before I could name it. My brothers and sisters and I wrote plays and musicals, created circuses, and built forts. We were an imaginative bunch. Imagination is the playground of creativity. Never forget that. Don't let your imagination lie fallow. That ground is rich and fertile for a storyteller, at no time more than when we are young and believe anything is possible. By keeping our imaginations active, by maintaining that sense of wonder, we writers continue to discover stories.

The memories of those early days shine brighter now than I know they were in reality. Over time our memories evolve to become stories we share with others—our children and grandchildren—to be passed down through the generations. I recall my third-grade year in Mrs. Crawford's class. She came to my desk, a story I'd written in her hands, and asked, "Mary Alice, did you ever think you might want to be a writer when you grow up?" I stared back at her, dumbfounded. I could get paid to write stories? As an eight-year-old child, I had never dreamed that writing could be a job. From that day forward, whenever I was asked what I wanted to be when I grew up, the answer came readily—a writer. Such is the power of a good teacher or mentor.

It would be decades before that tiny seed of possibility would grow and blossom into a career. I was not published at the tender age of seventeen and eighteen—the age of the students represented in this volume. At that age I had enough rejection slips from the magazine *Highlights for Children* to decorate a wall of my room. I learned early that rejection is a part of this career. I started out in journalism and later became a ghost writer for nonfiction books. My first novel didn't get published until well into my thirties. I lagged behind the pace of these brilliant young men and women.

They may be young, but these students have important things to say to the world. They are wise beyond their years and possess the talent to express themselves so clearly and with such voice that I was astonished. So pay attention to their short stories, poetry, and essays. Feel the emotions captured in words, rhymes, and diction. Hear the insights they've gleaned from their experiences and observations. Ponder their questions and opinions.

I encourage these young writers to keep writing. Stretch your writing muscles, challenge yourselves, enter more writing contests. Write as much as you can, as often as you can. Join writers' groups. Attend writing workshops and conferences. Keep putting your work out there to be reviewed and judged. Hone your craft. I still do, twenty-five years into my career. And I'll be honest, I still feel anxious when my work is reviewed. But it is just another part of the journey as a writer.

Allow me to pass on what I hope are helpful truths to this group of young writers:

- You are a writer because you are writing. Being published or not published doesn't define you as a writer.
- Share your work so it can be critiqued. And when you get the critiques back, set your ego aside. Don't be insulted by suggestions or corrections. Consider them. Your teachers, fellow writers, and, hopefully, agents and editor strive to help your book be the best it can be. But remember, in the end, it's your name on the piece of work.
- Winning or not winning contests does not define you as a writer.
- Keep learning. Expand your horizons. Don't allow yourself to be pigeonholed. Your writer's voice reflects who you are. Have something to say! When pursuing your careers, if you can't get the job you want, apply for one in the area of your chosen career. And then learn from it.

- Read! Read books and magazines. Read books in your favorite genre. Read books in all genres. Read cereal boxes, signs, and letters (other than texts and emails). Know your classics and catch up with contemporary authors.
- Obstacles in life are also opportunities. What you think is a bad turn of events may in fact be an opening to new possibilities.
- Say "Yes!" to those surprising opportunities that come your way.
- This is your life. Experience it fully. Be fearless. Find your voice. Create great memories. Be the hero in your own life's story.

Bravo to these brave, talented young writers. It was my great privilege to judge this body of work. And my great honor to introduce a new generation of America's thought-provoking, influential, informative, and entertaining writers in this collection: *Writing South Carolina.*

MARY ALICE MONROE

ACKNOWLEDGMENTS

It may take a village to raise a child, but to put on a statewide high-school writing contest takes a state. It takes a state of diligent, dedicated teachers to encourage their students to enter, and it takes a state of brave teenagers to put their young, fiercest thoughts out there in the world, exposed. We thank those teachers and realize we can't know how hard they work. And we thank those students, including those whose work wasn't selected for publication. Each had something interesting to say, and we learned from them all.

As with the previous two years, the topic is "How can we make South Carolina better?" High-school juniors and seniors are invited to respond in the genre of their choice—essay, poetry, drama, fiction—with the mandate not to exceed 750 words. Our panel of preliminary judges scores each entry—itself an interesting task—with the contest's founder, Steven Lynn, reading them the most carefully of all. This contest, and anthology series, is his baby. Steve's a curious, concerned English professor who wants many things, among them a better South Carolina and more competitions for young writers. Sparking the state's future leaders to think about improving their world is the kind of thing you'd expect from him, a Greer native and dean of the Honors College at the University of South Carolina. Partnering with the University of South Carolina Press, he and his staff presented a second round of writing competition on the USC campus in Columbia. Part field trip, part lunch-and-learn, this "Round 2" included the celebrity bonus of an acclaimed South Carolina writer speaking to the students. The writer—sometimes it's two—is that year's grand judge.

"She's so inspiring," we overheard students say after the vibrant, gracious Mary Alice Monroe spoke to them about how her career started, the lessons she's learned, the pain of being edited, and ways to get published. We thank Ms. Monroe. We also thank her assistant, Angela May. Their generosity and friendliness can't be overstated. And we empathize with Ms. Monroe's task of choosing the top three winners and honorable mentions in each class.

Round 2 includes the impromptu round. Finalists have forty minutes to respond to a question they've just heard. Ms. Monroe chose the topic, based loosely on her talk. "My novels are known for inspiring change in readers' lives—change in mind-set or habits—and calling them to action. What book has inspired change in your life or called you to action and why?" In this book you'll read the finalists' responses along with their initial submissions suggesting ways to make South Carolina better.

If students couldn't attend Round 2—think SAT, sickness, semesters abroad—individual teachers administered the impromptu topic. Our thanks to Kelly Minick at Saluda High, Heather Spittle at Nation Ford High in Fort Mill, Sarah Crist at St. James High in Murrells Inlet, Jessica Burke Stevens at Spartanburg High, Kristie Camp at Gaffney High, Bruno Rocha at Colegio Universo in Bom Despacho, Minas Gerais, Brazil, and Elise Hagstette at Heathwood Hall in Columbia.

Jonathan Haupt, former director, Linda Fogle, acting director, and Vicki Bates, their assistant, are our pillars at USC Press. They guide the book from contest to book creation. Merci, merci, merci.

Honors College English seniors James Bryan and Mae Bradford Howe took time from voracious school schedules to help with preliminary judging. Eleanor Mooney, an honors international studies freshman, also helped. Writer/editor Kathy Henry Dowell, who manages publications at USC's Thomas Cooper Library and formerly taught freshman English, lent her eye and experience to the submissions as well. We thank them and the staff at the Thomas Cooper Library, including Christine Nicol-Morris, Elizabeth Sudduth, and Robert Smith.

We're indebted to Thad Westbrook, the Honors College alumnus who generously funds the first-prize senior award and named it for Walter Edgar, his professor and noted South Carolina historian. We also thank the anonymous donor who funds the first-place junior prize and named it in memory of Dorothy Skelton Williams, an Anderson County educator who refused to believe any child couldn't learn.

Anthology editing and event planning are both wild ride and endurance test. Scrambling after teenagers—and their devices—is not for the easy quitter. But beyond the eye-opening and sometimes emotionally upsetting submissions we read, unexpected moments of courtesy and excitement reminded us this work isn't meaningless.

"Even though I wasn't one of the finalists, I just wanted to thank you for putting on this writing contest," a student emailed after her submission was declined. "I will continue to write, but most of all improve my writing." Then came this, from a student whose submission was accepted: "I appreciate the opportunity to participate in this event! Thank you for recognizing the importance of writing and listening to the voices of us young people."

She concluded with the colon and parenthesis— :) —to indicate she was smiling. And so were we.

Aïda Rogers

JUNIORS

Raising Violence

Alyssa Conner

You are young.
Loved by your mother and,
Eventually, by your father.
Love is inherited,
But respect is to be earned.
Ingrained into your head by your father's teachings.
"Only obey me and the teachings of God."
He always thought
You got along better with your mother.

You are ten.
After school one day, your father
Shows you his collection of rifles.
That was the same day you pushed a kid off the slide.
The day after you were kept awake
By your father's racist slurs as
He yelled at the television, his face
Illuminated by the light of the screen.
He looks at you with his small blue eyes and you
Force yourself to nod, out of
Some desperate hope to earn his respect.
He pats you on the shoulder.
Like a friend.
Like a father.
"This," he says, picking up a rifle,
     "Is a man's best friend."

You are thirteen.
Growing into adolescence, you begin to notice things
You never noticed before.
You begin taunting girls in your class—
A hobby that enables conversation between you and your father.
"That's my son," he says.
My son.
It was never "my son."
It was always "your son."
Never his.
Somewhere within you, you feel pride.
He lets you have a sip of his beer
That night.

You are fifteen.
You come home with a black eye.
"What happened, son?" your father asks.
"Just some kids," you say.
You father demands what happened.
You know your father wouldn't like the truth—
That you were bullied—he would think you were weak.
"I called some kids some mean words.
They didn't like it."
Your father can't hide his pride.
"Come here."
He takes you outside.
The sun stings your black eye
And you're almost thankful you can't see him that well.
"Hit me. Throw a punch."
You hesitate.
He slaps his chest, as if to demonstrate.
You throw a weak punch to his arm.
He grabs your fist.
"C'mon. Fight like a man. Not like a girl."
You hesitate.
And then you're throwing
Weak punches at his stomach.
And you can't hear his constant taunts
Because there's a ringing in your ears.

And tears in your eyes.
But you don't let him see.
You throw quick punches.
To make him feel pain—
To make him feel *your* pain—
He always did like
Your brother more.

You are sixteen.
Your past is behind you.
Your father gives you his old truck.
In the school parking lot,
You are the epitome of male masculinity.
That same year, you get your first girlfriend.
When you tell your father your girlfriend
Is coming over for dinner, he jokes,
"I'm just glad you're not gay.
Because if you were . . . we
Would have some problems."
You force a laugh and look away.
"She doesn't talk back does she?" he asks.
You shrug.
"You always gotta keep women in line."
He laughs. You don't.
The next day, he takes you on your first hunting trip.
You can't stop shaking for ten minutes
After shooting your first deer.
You're just glad your father
Didn't notice.

You are eighteen.
Your brother was accused of murdering his girlfriend.
The same month your dad hit your mother.
The same month your girlfriend broke up with you.
You think back to when you hit her
Earlier that month.
You were supposed to be the perfect
Southern gentleman, right?
You start to wonder

If things could have been different
If your brother's crime was just one of many—
A result of circumstance—
Feelings of hatred and dominance confused—
What would have happened if your father didn't
Give your brother one of his rifles?
If there was some way to prevent it.
And you start to wonder if your father was just
Raising violence.

*2.32 is the number**
2.32 per 100,000 women
Killed by men.
57 in 2013.
94 percent by those they knew.
We are the number one state in the country.
They are not numbers—they are humans
With lives.
And there are people with the power and tools to end them.

from a study conducted by the Violence Policy Center, using reports from 2013

Twenty-First-Century Pigeon House

Alyssa Conner

There is a certain tension that sometimes comes with assigned readings in school. It's usually a hit, a miss, or a juicy combination of both. For some odd reason, I've always found myself at the extreme side of either hit or miss, usually positioned against the majority. Sometimes when reading a book for class, I'll energetically talk about it to my friends, discussing my frustrations and quotes that struck a chord in me. Sometimes my friends will join in or scold me for spoiling them. I don't like class discussions. I don't like discussing novels with people I'm unfamiliar with. I have a need to test the terrain, toeing the line of the right answer and stating my personal opinion.

A book that has showed me the need for change is *The Awakening* by Kate Chopin. The novel was assigned reading for my sophomore AP language class. The book, simply judging from the cover, was disparate from all the other books we'd read that year. It depicted a woman's silhouette encased in a blue sheet of water. We'd read *The Scarlet Letter* earlier, which also featured a woman on the cover, except she was showcased in a materialistic light, cradling a child. But *The Awakening* was different. Not only because of the almost sensual feel of a woman's silhouette, but because a woman's name graced the cover.

Don't get me wrong, I've read novels for school written by women before. For example, *To Kill a Mockingbird* by Harper Lee. But while that story was told from the point of view of a youthful girl, it placed her father, Atticus Finch, at the forefront of the story. No one examined Scout's morality—she was just Atticus's daughter and drove his plot forward, almost a vehicle for the story. Atticus, however, was quiet yet firm and almost morally gray. *The Awakening,* on the other hand, detailed the inner conflict of a young, unhappy, and unsatisfied woman. Edna, the main character, was fully fleshed—she was logical yet also sensual and yearned for something more than her role as a wife and a mother. There was never a question of who the main character was; it was Edna, unrestrained from a central romantic plot line.

I wasn't completely inspired to change until after we'd finished the novel. Our teacher led us into a discussion-based activity she called "On the Fence." The rules were simple: we'd start in the middle of the classroom, she'd read a statement, and depending on if we agreed or disagreed with it, we would move to one side of the room. The idea was to convince those still on the fence to join your side.

My teacher read the first statement: "Edna was right in her decision to leave her husband." A large, almost appalling number of boys moved to the disagree side of the room.

"Edna's suicide at the end was her only option." The same boys shuffled to the other side, like it was a dance routine.

It was almost sickening how quickly the discussion of the novel became a battle of the sexes. The importance of the piece of literature was no longer in question. The discussion had turned to a fictional character's decision-making skills. The boys stood confidently, arms crossed over their chests, in their positions, while I wavered. I stumbled over my words, trying, and mostly failing, to express how astonished I was that a novel that was scandalous in the 1800s was still scandalous in the twenty-first century. How they thought the only solution for a struggling woman in society is death. They raised their voices, cutting me off, not waiting their turn to spit out their distaste for the book. The other girls in the classroom didn't seem all that eager to disagree, either. The boys hated Edna for the mere thought of leaving her husband for another man, which she never acted on and was never the main plot of the book, yet alone the most paramount. I was humbled. But I wasn't defeated.

I saw there needed to be change. I recognized the blind sexism in my own school. How boys tend to distance themselves from novels written from women's perspectives, despite the fact that a majority of novels we've read were written from men's perspectives and were still enjoyable, if not instant favorites, for the girls. Relatability isn't a strong enough excuse—I'm sure they couldn't relate to Huckleberry Finn, an adventurous, deeply southern boy who befriends a slave. And I'm sure Kate Chopin didn't write *The Awakening* for the sake of relatability to young men. She wrote it to express her desires, her fears—to present a realness to female characters that was absent in most literature at the time—something she probably couldn't do. Edna was jarringly realistic. The novel was driven by her thoughts and drastic impulses. It could've easily been categorized as a great, epic love story. But it wasn't. It was conscious.

The Awakening showed me the need for more female-driven and female-written literature assigned to us in school. We need more perspectives, more ideas—something I cautiously, yet proudly, hope to achieve through my own writing. But for now, we need assigned literature with more voices that extend beyond the usual stockpile of standards. More women's voices, more minority voices. William Shakespeare was a phenomenal playwright, but sometimes we need emotionally complex women that take center stage, as well.

Speaking for Those Too Young to Understand

Erin Hackney

Child abuse is a national calamity that is appalling and often draws violent and emotional reactions. South Carolina has improved in child well-being the last several years, and statistics from KIDS COUNT indicate we have risen from forty-fifth to forty-second in the nation for child well-being. While this is a step in the right direction, more can be done to save our innocent children from the atrocities of child abuse.

According to the South Carolina Department of Social Services, 37 percent of child abuse cases in 2011 resulted in no action being taken by the department, but in 2013 the percentage of cases where no action was taken dropped to 18 percent. This shows that DSS is becoming more proactive and perhaps points to more thorough investigations. However, that still leaves 2,938 out of 16,317 cases left with no action, and at least 2,938 children who are not protected. Whenever a child abuse case is reported to DSS, the response time varies from a couple of hours to a couple of days. Consistency with response times and thorough investigations could mean the difference between a child suffering for even a few more hours or in some cases days before DSS gets to them.

Unfortunately, I was a victim of child abuse. I was sexually abused by my grandfather for two years and also sexually abused every night for four months by my stepbrother. I finally spoke about it, at the age of twelve, to my friends one night at a sleepover and remember them asking if I was being molested. I did not even know what the term *molestation* meant. I do not remember getting any education about child abuse of any type except a coloring book I received in class one day in second grade that was about a little girl at the beach where an older man asked to touch her in her bathing suit area—the main point being "Say no and find a trusted adult." I did not link the coloring book to my situation. There should be more education for students and teachers after elementary school. I cannot recall a single lesson or guest speaker talking to us about signs, what the boundaries are, and where to go for help. If I had been more aware of the definition of child abuse, then I would have been able to understand the situation more clearly.

Children should know exactly what qualifies as child abuse and to whom they can go for support and advice, and they should be made well aware that no matter the circumstance, it is not their fault. Social media would be a great tool to use for this, because there is a diverse group of children on these websites. Having pages set up with a number for child abuse hotlines, FAQs about child abuse, and basic information on all types of child abuse can make a tremendous difference in the education of the community. South Carolina's deficient ranking in child welfare should make this state take steps immediately to address these issues and permeate the public with knowledge of abuse, the signs to look for, and how children may seek help. Schools should be required to implement more activities so kids understand that what is happening to them is actually abuse.

The children who are abused today are supposed to be the future of our state. We need to take better care of them. As a sixteen-year-old survivor of child abuse, I still struggle with the events of the past. I speak firsthand for the kids whose innocence is being ripped away before they even have a chance to understand life.

Works Cited

Children's Trust of South Carolina. "Frequently Asked Questions." 2015. Accessed 7 Oct. 2015.

Children's Trust of South Carolina. "If You Suspect Child Abuse or Neglect, Report It." 2015. Accessed 7 Oct. 2015.

Children's Trust of South Carolina. "Well-Being of South Carolina's Children." 2015. Accessed 7 Oct. 2015.

Gillum, Amber. "South Carolina Final Report on the FFY 2010–2014 Child and Family Services Plan." 30 June 2014. Accessed 7 Oct. 2015.

National Movement for America's Children. "Healthy Children, Healthy Communities." N.d. Accessed 7 Oct. 2015.

That One Line

Erin Hackney

A lot of books I read are just books for my own personal enjoyment. Though, as I reflect on those many books, I remember one that pulled me from the darkness that finds itself at home in my own mind. The name of that book is *Safe Haven* by Nicholas Sparks, and it saved me from thinking my sexual abuse was my own fault.

I was nine when the sexual abuse started with my grandfather, and I was eleven when it started with my stepbrother. I finally told my family about what was happening when I was twelve, about three to four months after my stepbrother had started. That is when the worst experience of my life began.

At age twelve I watched my parents cry and begin the battle for custody. My family split into a million pieces, and I got thrown into a room with a therapist who saw me only as another paycheck. All I could do was blame myself. I cried myself to sleep because some words I had said caused this. No matter how many times my therapist tried to shove down my throat that it was not my fault and I would get better, I still could not believe it. I could not believe because I had proof. Something I never told my parents, my therapist, my doctor, or my friends is that my body reacted to the touch of my stepbrother. My mind screamed "no!" but my body reacted. And it destroyed me.

It destroyed me until I read one line from *Safe Haven* that changed my view forever. The line that reads "and no matter how much I hated him, my nipples still hardened to his touch, and I hated my body for it." That one line showed me that not only was I not alone in my dark thoughts, but I truly was not at fault. A line from a book written by an author who will probably never know I existed saved me.

So now I finally put that dark thought to rest forever, as I finally write the one secret I never told anyone on paper for anyone and everyone to see. I finally put that dark thought to rest forever, as I finally state and truly believe

"I was the victim." I finally put that dark thought to rest forever, as I travel down the road to becoming a therapist, who does not see each child as a paycheck. But as someone whose profession and love are to save innocent souls, and put those dark thoughts that linger in children's heads to rest forever.

South Carolina, or,
A State of Improvement

Sydny Long

"How should we . . . what?"

I blinked uncomprehendingly. Surely, there was a missing element to the question, an essential detail my hasty eyes had discarded. To my dismay, the enclosed link divulged little more than entry rules and a dizzying amount of incentive that banished the mushrooming notion of indolence from my mind. Even if I didn't understand the prompt, such a lavish reward couldn't be dismissed. Not when my family depended on me to till the fields of scholarship opportunity and cultivate enough cash crops to fund my education.

Maybe I would put that in my essay. Everyone loved a sob story.

I read the prompt again, feeling justifiably frustrated. It was a trap. Was I expected to spew vituperatively about my home state? Or was I supposed to wax poetic about its pristine beaches and picturesque mountaintops? Was this an invitation to pull out my soapbox and preach our many sins? Was it an opportunity to be clever? Eloquent? Satirical? Grave?

Or, worst of all, was I supposed to be myself?

The mere concept was laughable. My writing was private, a proverbial secret garden where I fostered emotion and expression instead of posies and daisies. Every solitary word felt too exposed, too indicative of my true feelings. Even a scholarship essay would inevitably turn into a theatrical exploration of my unwanted opinions, opinions that likely would curl the lips of even the most progressive judges.

South Carolina. As I deliberated over the question, I realized I didn't know much about my home state. I lived near the border of North Carolina; most of my teachers and coaches were imported from Charlotte. Our annual vacation to Myrtle Beach and the occasional day trip to Columbia weren't enough for a decent perspective of the state. Those journeys were typically spent asleep at the window anyway.

I groped for even a vestigial image of South Carolina scenery and chanced upon perhaps my most unsavory memory. En route to the beach, we had passed through a town that had Confederate flags emblazoned across every storefront and suspended from the porch of every house. It had turned my stomach. Why did our state have to celebrate its troubled past? Why did we keep memorabilia of our slaveholding history? Why did we cling to the flag like it was something to be proud of?

That wasn't a vehicle for improvement, though. The only way to ameliorate the situation would be to tear down those ugly flags and watch them burn, but I knew this would only breed further dissent in the state. It was too aggressive an opinion to write about: knowing me, I would just descend into a senseless tirade about South Carolina's deeply racist roots. Be myself, indeed.

I thought again, this time focusing my efforts on education. My high school had recently been named one of the best in the nation, but South Carolina itself was consistently ranked as one of the worst states for education. How could I attend such an excellent school when children were receiving only the bare minimum a few districts over? School was so important to me and my future: why wasn't every student receiving the same opportunities?

I wanted to attend a good college. How could I when I didn't have a single decent idea for improvement? All I knew how to do was bring attention to the issues and wait idly for someone else to contrive a solution.

And then I unlocked the enigma behind the prompt. This *was* the improvement.

By encouraging students to evaluate the flaws of their own state, South Carolina was learning to assess its own weaknesses. The prompt was asking us—the future leaders of the world—to cultivate an awareness and share our grievances in the hopes it would ignite a passion. *We were the improvement.* We were the complexes waiting to be activated. We were the cause for change.

As I exited out of the webpage, I reluctantly realized that my perception of the prompt might not be shared by the judges. I wasn't really answering the question in an orthodox manner. But I wasn't discouraged: I had deciphered the prompt, and I was freshly motivated to write. South Carolina wasn't a perfect state, but it was still mine and I still had the means to improve it.

I opened my Word program and began to write.

The Words That Wouldn't Come Out

Sydny Long

My mother's pearls of wisdom could have crafted the longest, finest necklace of such baubles in the world. She bequeathed her various dicta to me with the confidence that I would guard these pearls and—one distant day—string them together for my own child. And cherish them I did, tucking each brilliant gem into the jewelry box of my mind where such treasures could never be stolen away by the greedy fists of dementia.

With one exception.

There were particular books in my middle school library that I was not to check out. "They're too mature for you," my mother would say, already scanning my expression for a fleeting glimmer of dissent. "You need to be a child for as long as you can. Don't read them, baby." I nodded then, her docile little girl.

The very next week, I plucked a particular novel off the shelf, promptly buried it under binders and vocabulary folders, and entered the world of adolescent rebellion.

I had always been a dutiful child, conditioned into placidity by incentives and fear of consequences. My secret allowed me a taste of disobedience, a dollop of its fiery broth. I remained electrified by my actions as I hid myself in my closet and opened the novel that would one day instill me with the strength to speak.

The book—*Speak* by Laurie Halse Andersen—revolved around a high school student who lost her friends, her motivation, and her voice to a summertime mishap. Melissa had been raped by a classmate at a party; her call for help inadvertently summoned the police and got a few partygoers arrested for alcohol possession. Their animosity toward her only clad the walls around her heart in iron and facilitated her penchant for keeping to herself. It wasn't until the rapist attempted to assault her again that Melissa finally unearthed the voice she had buried so long ago and learned to speak again.

I was slightly terrified by the premise, but the novel enlightened rather than frightened me. All the nebulous discussions of rape and assault had been kept covert by uptight parents and cautious teachers, a subject not to be approached and never to be discussed. Due to the infrequency of discussion, I assumed rape and assault a harmless rarity that struck only the women with the lowest-cut necklines and the highest blood alcohol counts.

Speak, however, blasted the ignorance from my mind like an earthbound icicle, leaving piercing clarity in its wake. Melissa had been an artistic, outgoing girl, a child in some regards, and she had been viciously attacked for no reason other than she was within arm's reach. My younger self was horrified, of course, but she still did not comprehend the devastating repercussions of such a crime. That knowledge, however, should never have been foisted upon her.

When I was fifteen, I was sexually assaulted by my then-boyfriend. The event was so entrenched in normalcy—the fleece of my favorite blanket, the reverberation of the speakers rhapsodizing in the key of static, the filmy heat of pasta cooking—so much so that I believed it was appropriate for our three-month relationship. My mind snatched up the incident and enshrouded it in the muslin sheets of repression.

It wasn't until I saw a copy of *Speak* in a local bookshop that the smothered memory emerged. All of this time I had been emulating Melissa: burying my emotions, retreating into the dreary solitude of my wounded soul, drifting through the motions with little regard for what I encountered along the way. I found my voice again that day and now I present it proudly. I boast my ability to speak freely, to stand up for those who haven't recovered their own voices yet, and to say "no" when I mean it.

Some books stay with us. Others, however, leave not an impression, but a gift. We may not appreciate the gifts we are given, but they affect us nonetheless, and once the time is right, we can peel back the paper and finally see what we were missing. My mother's pearls may grace my neck, but Anderson's *Speak* graces my mind by forever altering my perceptions and—eventually—saving my life.

Teenage Roulette

Sarah Finleyson

One in three girls in South Carolina get pregnant as a teenager, and statistics show that four of the twelve girls in my English class will be responsible for another human life before their twenty-first birthday. Of those four, two will go on to earn a high school diploma, and none will likely graduate from college. South Carolina ranks twelfth out of fifty for the highest number of births to teens ages fifteen to nineteen. Pregnancy among teenagers is a critical issue in our state that continues to affect the brightest of the next generation, and it's a problem that can no longer be ignored because of religious values or political agendas. Reducing the number of teen pregnancies starts with reforming our sexual education in schools, allowing greater access to low-cost contraceptives and birth control, and providing substantially more support and training for teenage mothers.

South Carolina's sex education relies on the outdated notion that teens will abstain from sex until marriage. This is not the case. More than half of all teenagers in South Carolina have sexual intercourse while in high school. In fact 21 percent of these sexually active students say they have had four or more partners ("South Carolina Adolescent Reproductive Health Facts"). Yet when it comes to sex ed, the state chooses to focus on shamebased abstinence programs that result in a mixed cocktail of confusion, humiliation, and degradation, leading many teens to be suspicious of all sexual health educators. Thus they take matters into their own hands for contraception, which includes very little, if any at all. Because the pseudoscience used in these sexual education curriculums preaches that birth control is ineffective, condom use has decreased 9 percent in recent years statewide, and only 17 percent of South Carolina teens say they are on birth control (CulpRessler). Unless South

Carolina acknowledges that teenagers have sex and implements progressive, prevention-oriented education, the well-meaning abstinence-promoting programs will continue to metastasize and give way to a generation of unprepared and unaware teenagers.

If teens decide to venture outside of school for contraceptive advice, there are few clinics that provide low-cost medical care, birth control, free contraceptives, and emergency actions such as abortion. Planned Parenthood has only two clinics in South Carolina, and after recent events concerning the federal government funding of Planned Parenthood, the addition of clinics is doubtful. Unfortunately the counties that need these services most are woefully far from any such providers. Rural counties in South Carolina have the highest number of teenage pregnancies, yet the lowest number of outreach programs to combat this problem. The societal stigma of adolescent sex discourages teens from talking to parents or family members about prevention, and the lack of reliable health clinics often drives teens to play a pregnancy roulette. The cost of installing affordable health clinics around the state is nominal compared to the taxes South Carolinians already are paying: there is a staggering $166 million in costs associated with teen pregnancy ("State Facts about Unintended Pregnancy"). Creating more contraceptive dispensaries also reduces the funding for abortion clinics, because the more prevention is practiced, the fewer unplanned pregnancies will occur.

Once a teen becomes pregnant, the outcome can be tragic. Fifty percent of teen moms do not graduate from high school, and teen fathers are 30 percent less likely to graduate ("Adverse Effects"). This translates into higher unemployment and poverty among teenage parents, therefore placing the burden of supporting them on the child welfare system and government-assisted programs. Allendale County has the highest teen pregnancy rates, and 56.1 percent of children born to teenage mothers in that county live in poverty ("Selected Indicators"). By providing these mothers with educational and vocational training, they could compete in the workforce and better provide for their young families. With affordable, high-quality child care, teen mothers can work while their children are being prepared to enter schools, laying the foundation for successful citizens and breaking the cycle of teenage pregnancy and poverty among these families.

On the whole, the blatant inadequacies in South Carolina's sexual education program must be rectified, the availability of low-cost contraceptives and health services must increase, and the sordid tradition of teen pregnancy and poverty in families must be ameliorated. The next generation of South Carolinians can pave the way for thriving communities. The travesty of allowing the current situation to exist without reform ensures calamity now, and nothing but catastrophe for the future.

Works Cited

CulpRessler, Tara. "Since Most South Carolina School Districts Aren't Following Sex Ed Laws, Fewer Teens Are Using Condoms." ThinkProgress.org. 16 Jan. 2013.

———. 2005–2015 Center for American Progress Action Fund. 16 Jan. 2013. Accessed 28 Oct. 2015.

Kids Count Data Center. "Selected Indicators for Allendale County." Anne E. Casey Foundation. 2014. Accessed 29 Oct. 2015.

Office of Adolescent Health. "South Carolina Adolescent Reproductive Health Facts." US Department of Health and Human Services. 2011. Accessed 29 Oct. 2015.

South Carolina Campaign to Prevent Teen Pregnancy. "State Facts about Unintended Pregnancy: South Carolina." National Campaign to Prevent Teen and Unplanned Pregnancy. Apr. 2014. Accessed 29 Oct. 2015.

Youth.gov. "Adverse Effects." 2012. Accessed 29 Oct. 2015.

Cheer Up

Sarah Finleyson

As my mother glanced at the title of the book that had rarely left my side the past few days, she offhandedly remarked, "Oh, that will cheer you up!" She couldn't have been further from the truth. *It's Kind of a Funny Story* by Ned Vizzini is not the sort of novel people turn to when they are looking for an escape from the inexplicable heaviness of everyday life. In fact, it's the frank and honest perception of those topics we would like to avoid, such as depression, drinking, and drugs—all the less favorable realities of being a teenager—that initially drew me in to the book.

I first started reading the novel because I was sad, and that, in essence, is what Vizzini's book is about: a teenager who is sad. Except his sadness is not really sadness at all, it's a different beast entirely. One that controls you like a puppet master controls his marionette. It's about a boy with depression who is manipulated by his brain chemistry's invisible strings. A boy who can no longer eat, or sleep, or have normal interactions because the tentacles and pressures to get Good Grades in order to get into a Good College, which leads to having a Good Job and results in a comfortable Good Life, have overwhelmed him. Teenagers have so many variables throwing themselves in our paths, begging us to make a decision and put our lives' prosperity on the line. The way the world is designed now, a single B in calculus could seemingly ruin your whole future. This feeling of being thrown into the middle of the ocean and expected to find the shore is portrayed so accurately that it was a relief. A relief to know I am not alone in my panic.

It's Kind of a Funny Story's relatability is what drew me in, but its portrayal of events happening to those closest to me is what kept me entranced. About the time I was old enough to recognize the term *depression* but not old enough to know why it made my mom cry every night or burned her into an emotionally drained shadow of her former self, my mother received a diagnosis:

depression. I had never understood what depression was. I, like the rest of my uninformed friends and family, thought it was something she could just snap out of. When she didn't, I blamed myself for not doing more as a daughter—more drawings, more jokes, more hugs; I would do more of anything to make her smile.

Some years later, when I first opened my copy of Vizzini's novel, I learned why I was never enough. Depression is not simply having a bad day, not simply making the decision to eat or to get out of bed, or smile. No amount of willpower can fix a chemical imbalance, a disease of the mind. Depression is a chemical imbalance of the brain, and genetics play a role, and through this book, I finally understood the feelings of my mother. Since then it seems as though a weight has been lifted off of my shoulders, not because the mood swings have lessened or the bad days spontaneously got better, but because *It's Kind of a Funny Story* gave me the answers to the what and the why of her own feelings and my own. It existed as a flame that illuminated and eliminated the darkest fear of all—the fear of the unknown.

So, Mother, Ned Vizzini's book did not cheer me up, but it made me understand how you felt, and that has made all the difference.

Simple Solutions

Alaina Kiffer

The state of South Carolina has the potential to become one of the greatest states in the United States, but it has a long way to go before it reaches that point. One of the ways this goal could be achieved would be by requiring regular auto inspections, improving roads, and increasing the age requirement for people to get their driver's licenses.

An average of 863 traffic deaths occurred annually in South Carolina from 2008 to 2012, according to TRIP, a national transportation research group, and during that time South Carolina was tied for the highest fatality rate in the nation. Thankfully that number has gone down somewhat. In 2014, the state highway patrol reported 823 traffic fatalities, and as of late 2015, it reported 788. This number is still elevated when one considers that the state of New York—which, according to a 2014 census, has a population of 19.75 million compared to South Carolina's 4.832 million—only had 966 fatalities in 2014, according to a report by the New York DMV's 2014 Statewide Statistical Summary. Based on calculations, .005 percent of New York's population was killed in a car crash, while .014 percent of South Carolina's population was killed in a car crash. As reported in "The Most Deadly Driving States in America," an article in a 2015 issue of *Business Insider* magazine, South Carolina is still one of the worst states for fatal car crashes, while New York is the third-safest state to drive in.

One may ask why the state of South Carolina is so dangerous when it does not have harsh winters with extreme road conditions or a high population density like New York, Ohio, and many other northern and northwestern states. I think part of the answer is rather simple. South Carolina does not require regular auto inspections—New York does—and overall lacks preventative maintenance that would make South Carolina a safer, more productive, and less expensive state to live in. The lack of safety inspections means that many cars do not have proper brakes, proper tire tread, working headlights, or other very important safety features. These features exist for a reason and could very well make all the difference in a life-or-death situation. Improper tire tread can lead to hydroplaning, improper brakes can lead to a failure to stop, and a headlight out could mean another driver does not see someone and hits them. These are just a few of the problems that could arise simply because people are not forced to do regular maintenance on their cars and get regular vehicle inspections.

Another problem is with South Carolina's roads themselves. "South Carolina roadways lack some desirable safety features, have inadequate capacity to meet travel demands, or have poor pavement conditions," TRIP reports. These problems cost residents "approximately $3 billion annually in the form of additional vehicle costs, lost time, and wasted fuel due to traffic congestion and traffic crashes," TRIP continues. Just a bit more spending on the state's part would save so much time, money, and even lives.

Additionally South Carolina could decrease the number of fatal car crashes by increasing the age requirements to drive and the rigor to get a license. Driving is a privilege, not a right, and it needs to be treated as such. At age fifteen, South Carolinians are allowed to get a provisional license, and at seventeen they can get a regular driver's license without taking driver's education courses. At fifteen, most teenagers are not mature enough to handle the responsibility of driving, and the lack of rigor required to pass driving exams allows inexperienced and poorly trained drivers on the road, where they often become a hazard. Not surprisingly the safest states to drive in—Massachusetts, New York, Rhode Island, and New Jersey—all require driver's education courses to obtain an unrestricted driver's license before the age of eighteen. None of those states allow teenagers to begin driving until they are sixteen, according to dmv.org. This is clear proof that the requirements for obtaining a license need to be made more rigorous and the age requirements should be raised. The slight inconvenience is well worth making roads safer and saving lives, especially when one considers the fact that car crashes are the leading cause of teenage deaths, according to the Centers for Disease Control and Prevention.

Increasing the age requirement and rigor for obtaining a license, improving roads, and requiring regular auto inspections: simple changes that could save so many and improve so much.

Krasivaya

Alaina Kiffer

Causing change. Perhaps that is why every author writes. Perhaps that is why every musician goes out there and makes music. Perhaps that is why every actor goes out there and pours their heart and soul into becoming someone else. Enacting change certainly is a noble cause—one that every person can, and should aspire to.

To be touched by someone else's work is likely one of the most satisfying and wonderful feelings you can ever have, and you can be certain many books and stories have shaped our lives. The written word has been powerful enough to topple regimes and cause dictators to tremble in their boots, and that is because words speak to people in a way one can only dream of.

Many books have touched me at one point or another. My very first book, *Dick and Jane,* taught me how to read, and is to this day a cherished gift from my grandmother. The *Pine Hollow* stories by Bonnie Bryant were the very first books I ever cried over. Then there was *Crime and Punishment,* which nearly drove me insane and which I could read only a few pages at a time because it was so laborious. *Stories for a Kindred Heart* brought me comfort when I moved from New York to South Carolina and left my friends behind and saw me through the dark days of my grandmother's death.

One novel has spoken to me in a way no other has ever done. Many times I have had to stop reading it because I could no longer see the pages through my haze of tears. *Between Shades of Gray* by Ruta Sepetys follows Lina, a young girl in Lithuania during the Soviet occupation, and her arduous journey to a Siberian gulag, all because her father was considered a threat. It tells of a woman who gives birth to a baby and is immediately taken from the hospital and sent to Siberia. That baby dies before it ever gets a chance at life. It tells the story of people facing unimaginable suffering, and yet they remain strong throughout it all and the human spirit rises above their circumstances. It tells the power of art and music to bring people hope even in the darkest of times.

This novel has filled me with an unimaginable sense of rage toward the perpetrators of these acts, and the strongest sense of injustice I have felt since I first saw a video of the 9/11 attack in fifth grade. You may ask how this book could have changed my life when it is based on something so long ago and is nothing like what I am dealing with in my own life. This is a story that transcends time and space and serves as a warning. *Between Shades of Gray* is set during World War II. If you read any history books, you will find they focus almost solely on Nazi Germany and the Holocaust. The Soviet Union's barbarous treatment of Lithuanians, Finns, and even their own citizens is virtually ignored. We have forgotten thousands upon thousands of people who suffered just as much as the Jews in Nazi Germany. We have allowed the Lithuanians and Finns to become lost in the folds of history, and they must be brought to light. They must be honored and not forgotten; to allow them to be forgotten would be a sin.

Because of this novel, I intend to make their story known to as many people as I can, and to do so by any means possible. I want to research their story more and write my own book about them, fiction or nonfiction. Perhaps I will even write a book that goes through many examples of man's injustice toward his own kind in hopes it will spur people to action. That is the root of every injustice committed: passive inaction. As a musician, I also would like to write a song to honor those who have suffered and warn listeners of what can happen. I would also like to become more involved in politics in the future so that I may be able to enact change across the nation and help prevent future atrocities.

Between Shades of Gray showed me one can never turn a blind eye toward evil. The United States had the opportunity to save the people being shipped to Siberia to suffer and die but, because the Soviet Union was an ally, allowed those atrocious acts to continue. The United States chose to focus on Hitler and ignore the suffering of thousands more, and only then because we were attacked at Pearl Harbor and realized we could no longer stuff our heads into the sand and pretend the war did not affect us.

Injustice should never be tolerated. Human suffering should never be tolerated. We should never turn away and say, "It's not my problem," when we see our fellow man in pain. Not only does this apply at an international and national level, it applies to our everyday lives. It is our duty as human beings to help our fellow man. It is our duty to bring about change in our world and to keep making it the best that it can be, one person at a time.

The "S" Word

Bailey Babb

High school is hard enough with upcoming tests, pop quizzes, and maintaining a social life. Attempting to balance the daily trials of a student while simultaneously carrying and caring for a baby is incomprehensible. The four years spent in high school should be focused on education and the exploration of personal growth, relationships, and future goals. This essential time of development should not be delayed by the massive responsibility of parenthood. Unfortunately this will become the terrifying new reality for more than four thousand teenage girls this year in the state of South Carolina, according to a 2013 study by the South Carolina Campaign to Prevent Teen Pregnancy.

To put the entirety of the blame upon these girls is unreasonable. For the most part, effective education tends to suffice when teaching correct methods. Math teachers, regardless of whether their students will use complicated formulas in their lives, still go in-depth to make sure their students understand how to solve a problem. Why is this mindset not applied to sexual education? Obviously not everyone who takes sex ed will become sexually active, just like not everyone who takes calculus will become a mathematician. So where exactly is the hesitation in teaching a realistic approach to sex?

Perhaps the hesitation comes from the word itself. The word *sex,* especially in the South, is taboo, almost to a point of absurdity. A seed is planted early in young children's minds that sex is a forbidden topic. Bringing it up to anyone will most likely be answered with either giggles or a look of disgust. Children witness how the adults in their lives handle the pressures of sex in different forms. If a sex scene comes up in a movie, adults will typically cover their children's eyes. If there's a dirty joke, adults for the most part shy away from explaining it to their children and attempt to temper their own laughter. Regardless of whether adults are right in doing so or not, it puts the idea in kids' minds that sex is a topic that is not on the table for discussion.

Fast forward to the teenage years, and those kids find that sex is a reality. It's no longer a scene in a movie or a dirty joke. They have been taught to shy away from discussions about sex, but it is almost unavoidable. If they do not feel comfortable talking to a family member, they are likely to turn to friends. And if that is not bad enough, the one class they have revolving around the subject has been reduced to only teaching about abstinence—not birth control, teen pregnancy, or proper sexual relationships. Absurdity rules in high school, but it is in the curriculum now, not the gossipy girls or minidramas in the hallways.

This seems to be an unfortunate cycle for many teenagers. They find themselves too embarrassed to talk to parents, afraid of being shut down by their teachers, and by default, forced to talk to people who are just as confused as they are. The best solution has to be replacing abstinence-only education with a comprehensive approach to sex education. We need a class where information is clear, prevention methods are explained thoroughly, and questions can be asked without students feeling guilty for being confused. We need a sexual education class that actually discusses sex.

Of course, switching from abstinence-only education to a practical class will not fix the entirety of the issues. Honestly, by the time students enter sexual education classes, they already have a pretty clear idea of what they will or will not do, and for some, it is too late to change their minds. Teenagers will continue to refuse safety measures or will not care enough to take precautions. Mistakes will inevitably happen. At least this way, with a better foundation of knowledge, teens will be realistically prepared to face the challenges that come with sexual activity.

It is time for a change. The state board of education, local school districts, and the state legislature can pretend the "if we don't talk about it, it doesn't exist" method works, but back in reality, 48 percent of high school students admit to being sexually active, according to the National Campaign to Prevent Teen and Unplanned Pregnancy. State officials can only pretend for so long. While they enjoy their fantasy, teen moms are dropping out of high school, are struggling to find work, and are at home just as confused as they were before.

Works Cited

"South Carolina: The National Campaign." South Carolina: The National Campaign. https://powertodecide.org/what-we-do/information/national-state-data/national. Accessed 2 Nov. 2015.

South Carolina Campaign to Prevent Teen Pregnancy. "Half Way There: Teen Pregnancy in South Carolina." 2014. Accessed 2 Nov. 2015.

I Believe in Magic

Bailey Babb

There's always been something comforting about reading. Books are like old friends. They're there to help you forget about the day-to-day, teach you some valuable advice, and inspire you to be the best you can be. For me *Harry Potter and the Deathly Hallows,* by J. K. Rowling, did just that.

I can honestly say I've never fallen so deeply in love with a story as I have with the Harry Potter series. It offered a way not only to escape this world, but to enter an entirely new universe full of magic and mythical creatures and outlandish characters. The final book in the series, *The Deathly Hallows,* wrapped all of the twists, turns, characters, and themes together into a perfect conclusion. This mastery of storytelling, as exemplified by J. K. Rowling, taught me that it is completely possible to write a complex story while not losing track of the principles upon which your story is based.

In *The Deathly Hallows,* Harry, Hermione, and Ron face seemingly impossible challenges. To take down Voldemort—a dark and powerful wizard—they must abandon their last year of school, leave their families, and continuously risk their lives to protect themselves, each other, and other innocent lives. Through these hardships, Rowling develops an important lesson: life is not easy. Granted, reality's difficulties don't necessarily consist of battling evil wizards, but there are bad people who try to hurt us. And sometimes problems can seem impossible. *The Deathly Hallows* teaches that if you surround yourself with loyal friends, accept challenges, and are willing to make sacrifices, you can overcome anything. And as portrayed in the concluding chapters, you might not have a perfect fairy-tale ending. But doing the right thing is worth it.

Perhaps above all, *The Deathly Hallows* taught me to stay true to myself and my friends. In the hardest of times, I often forget to ask myself what's best not only for me, but for the people surrounding me. Now I know to turn to my friends. They are always willing to lend advice or offer to help in any way they can. When I'm too scared to take a risk, they encourage me to have more faith and reassure me they will continue to support me, even if something goes wrong.

And yes, Rowling understood friendship is complex and fragile at times. She had an answer for that too. No matter how many times fights lead to an estrangement, if they're truly your friends, they'll come back. In *The Deathly Hallows,* Harry and his best friend, Ron, get into a fight, leading Ron to abandon the mission and go back home. Like Harry and Ron, I have often gotten into petty arguments with friends. However, just like in the books, real friends realize the fight is not worth the destruction of a friendship. They will return, apologies will be shared, and the past will become the past.

When I began reading the Harry Potter series, I never imagined it would impact my life the way it has. Rowling's seamless storytelling managed to keep me entertained enough to reread the series over and over, teach me something new about life with every new character, chapter, and adventure, and maybe most important, inspire me to be the best writer I can be. Great writing isn't just putting words on paper. It's taking the reader on a magical adventure. It's making characters as real as you and me. It's creating worlds between "once upon a time" and "the end."

I believe in magic. Not because Harry Potter had a wand, but because J. K. Rowling had a pen.

The Decrescendo of the Arts

Candace Beebe

When Nikki Haley was elected to the governor's office in 2012, she immediately began an effort to provide tax relief for the citizens of South Carolina. As a result she vetoed eighty-one bills that tallied up to $67.5 million during her first term. She discarded funding for many programs she deemed to be "wasteful local projects." When Governor Haley cut those "wasteful projects," she cut fine arts funding.

However, taking away funding for the arts proved the importance of them. Fine arts can improve overall grades, quality of life, and even mental health. In a study done by the Kennedy Center, students involved in the arts are more likely to stay in school, pay attention in class, have better behavior and attitudes, and make better grades. There was also an inquiry done in 2005 by the College Board that shows students with four years or more of involvement with a fine arts program scored up to twenty-five points higher on the SAT than their peers. Both studies show that music intrinsically helps focus the mind and that classes in the fine arts spectrum actually can have an impact on students' core classes, as measured by standardized testing.

Yet, there are more than just numbers on a test to prove how meaningful fine arts programs are for students. These classes give students a way to escape the cookie-cutter world. They open a door to escape the monotony of everyday subjects that are important but often pigeonhole students and do not often lend themselves to creative expression. However, walk into a music room and watch students blaze their own trails as they mix their individual parts together to showcase their talent as the group blends in perfect harmony. The arts create their own rules. In the robotic world in which we live today, children should be taught to ask questions and find answers on their own; they should question everything to better understand the world and its beauty and abstract wonder. Performing arts create the inspiration and passion to discover and enjoy the more intricate parts of life as the whole world speeds by in our fast-paced society.

Fine arts can also be used to help struggling or at-risk kids. Programs like band, orchestra, art, theater, and chorus are considered of great importance in community organizations like the Boys and Girls Clubs, the YMCA, and after-school programs. These groups keep children out of trouble, off the street, and on a path to a bright future. Specifically, lost and hurting high-school freshmen join the band only to get their fine art credit but find a family and a purpose through music. Band provides identity. Band provides an instrument to enhance their self-infused passion and direct it toward one common goal, greatness. Band causes one to examine and reflect through music, which bleeds into other areas of life. This has been the case for me these last six years in the band. They are my family, sometimes my purpose for coming to school, and always a place where I can be myself.

Music has always been a fundamental part of humanity. Since the beginning of time, people have used music in all areas of their lives. Humanity craves music because the right hemisphere of the brain houses rhythm and creativity. Music decreases stress and anxiety levels, changes the heart rate, and can help an infant's eating habits, reports Dr. Joseph Mercola in his article "Listening to Music Prompts Numerous Brain Changes." Music has such a powerful impact that forty American soldiers with major PTSD symptoms were given a guitar, sheet music, and weekly lessons for six weeks. Results show the music was effective in reducing their symptoms of depression and improving their health-related quality of life (Health Services Research and Development).

What would improve South Carolina would be not to take away the arts but to support them more. Even hinting at getting rid of these programs is profane. Band has made my middle and high school career more enjoyable. Band has encouraged me to think outside the box and accept challenges I might otherwise not have the courage to tackle. Band is who I am. After all, music makes the world a better place.

Works Cited

Bowers, Paul. "Haley Vetoes Spending for Education, Healthcare, Arts." *Charleston (S.C.) City Paper.* 6 July 2012. Accessed 2 Nov. 2015.

Health Services Research and Development. "Music Therapy Program Helps Relieve PTSD Symptoms." 6 Jan. 2014. Accessed 2 Nov. 2015.

Institute of Education Sciences. *Critical Evidence: How the Arts Benefit Student Achievement.* N.d. Accessed 2 Nov. 2015.

Jamiecarr. "SC Gov. Nikki Haley Completely Cuts Funding to the SC Arts Commission." CNN iReport. 8 July 2012. Accessed 2 Nov. 2015.

Mercola, Joseph. "Why Your Brain Craves Music." Mercola.com. 26 Apr. 2013. Accessed 2 Nov. 2015.

Turner, Judith. "General Effects of Music Therapy, How Music Therapy Is Used." *Psychology Encyclopedia.* N.d. Accessed 2 Nov. 2015.

The Power of the Written Word

Candace Beebe

Life as a teenager can be a funny thing. Your parents and elders tell you it should be the best time of your life—a time to live, learn, and explore. However, my experience being a teenager and going through high school has been more of a monotonous journey, doing the same thing day after day. It can be boring, and I find myself becoming complacent and satisfied with where I am, which is not who I want to be. I want to be the kind of person who continually pushes myself to the next level. I always want to strive to be better tomorrow than I am today, so when I read *The Great Gatsby* by F. Scott Fitzgerald my sophomore year, it truly spoke to me.

At the beginning of the book, I felt that I was most like Nick Carraway, the narrator, trying to find his way through life. He wasn't really sure who to be or what to do. He had graduated from Yale University and even fought in World War I, but even with those great accomplishments he still felt lost. Nick was from a good family and had good friends but never felt like he fit in, so he moved from Minnesota to right outside of New York City, the heart of the 1920s. I thought I was most like him, trying to find my place in a world full of open doors and paths but unsure of which to take. Like Nick, I put myself where I thought I'd figure out my future but instead figured out something else.

After Nick moved to New York, he met Jay Gatsby. He found someone who looked perfect, as if he had it all together, when in reality he had an inner war raging. Gatsby looked great from the outside—rich, handsome, and a little mysterious. But then you learn of his passionate love for a married woman. He'd always been in love with her, but she had forgotten him. So his forbidden love for her grew inside his heart and mind. We then learn that all of Gatsby's wealth was acquired for the sole purpose of "winning" Daisy back. All he wanted to do was live his life to please her. He found her and moved across the country where she was and even bought the house right across from hers. Then he'd throw elaborate parties hoping that one day by chance she would walk in. She was his passion, his inspiration, his muse. At this point of the story, I realized I didn't want to be like Nick, but I hoped to be more like Gatsby—a man who follows his heart and goes after his inspiration with everything he had within himself. He gave his life so that he might make her love him again.

I realize *The Great Gatsby* is fiction. I understand that this didn't really happen, and even if it did, it didn't work out well for Gatsby in the end anyway. But within Gatsby's love and passion, I found my own. It changed me. I no longer was satisfied with where I was. I wanted to chase something with every fiber in my being. I want to be so inspired that even I couldn't talk myself out of it. I wanted excitement and drive. Gatsby wasn't afraid, he wasn't anything except determined and eager to see all of his dreams come true.

After we finished *The Great Gatsby*, I finally decided to take the Advanced Placement English language and composition course. I also decided that one day I wanted to become an English teacher myself. I realized that reading and writing are my passions, and I want to share them with others and pass them on to the generations after me, so the love of literature will never be lost or taken for granted. I love to read, for the power words have to change a person's mind to become whatever and whoever they want to be is indescribable. How a word or sentence can be the inspiration to flip a person's whole world is mind-boggling. This book caused me to be a better person and taught me I didn't have to be perfect or even wildly accomplished to succeed.

Deep inside Gatsby was a regular person who was in love and stopped at nothing to achieve his goals. Gatsby inspired me to not be average but to be someone deeply inspired and determined to take chances and live life to its full potential.

The New Renaissance

Issac Blackwell

What if Einstein's education funding had been cut at a young age,
In favor of the kids who were the easiest to teach;
What if Voltaire, the founder of freedom of expression, was
Silenced by teachers wanting to make everything orderly and uniform?

What if Freud were structured to go into the wool business like his father
So that he would have never gone on to found the field of psychoanalysis;
What if Mozart's prodigal music ability had been replaced with
The skills needed just for succeeding in a program developed by people
    with suits
as gray as their jobs, and mind-set?
What if Kant was taught to have just
Enough mental capacity for multiple choice questions, and not push
the boundaries of philosophy and question human ethics?
What if Archimedes had to follow an already established and overly
    complicated way of
Making sure it was really Hiero's Crown, instead of being creative and
    discovering water's property of
Displacement?

What if da Vinci was too worried about his overly structured and systemized
    grading systems that,
In his diary, it was full of the pressure that is piled on him by subjects he
    finds boring and useless?
What if Darwin was required to accept the sciences of the time, and could
    not

Deviate from these "laws" that do not leave much for the imagination?
What if Picasso had his art set replaced with a textbook, and his
Easel with lined paper in his early years?
What if Franklin was coddled as a child
And was deterred from his eureka in the electrical storm?
What if Shakespeare was too busy with scientific busy work that he could not
Learn and experiment with the English language itself?

What if we shaped our children into spheres, rather than boxes?
Well-rounded and full, rather than confined and empty inside.
What if we called these men what they really were,
Not scientists or philosophers, or even doctors, but rather artists?
What if we could start a rebirth of art in our youth,
by asking "why not?" instead

?

A Grave Understanding

Issac Blackwell

When I was younger, I would devour books. My mom would have to shovel in several books at a time to fuel the steam train that was my growing mind. I remember one book in particular, *The Graveyard Book* by Neil Gaiman. At first glance this was above my knowledge base, although I read about many topics that might not have been studied as a fourth or fifth grader. *The Graveyard Book* was about this young boy who was given the name Nobody by a ghost couple who found him after his entire family was murdered. Despite the fact that he knew magic and could travel into other dimensions, I could connect with this boy, this Nobody. I too had experienced loss, specifically family, and it has made me feel hollow even to this day. Tears form as I think about it, but thanks to this dark-haired, odd, and very pale boy, the pain I have is no longer as piercing.

This book taught me it was okay to be different, that everyone has at one point been a "Nobody," that you can get past the hopelessness. In this book Nobody grew to be a very kind and gentle boy, despite having been through the death of his family and being raised by the inhabitants of a graveyard. *The Graveyard Book* taught me there is light and dark inside of everyone, but it is how you channel these forces inside you that make you who you are, that define you. Not your past.

Some people choose to let their darkness fester inside them, letting it rot their hearts until they are a shell of what they once were. Such was the man who killed Nobody's family, all for the betterment of his organization. You can see it today with mass shootings and bombings. These are instances where these troubled beings' inner darkness, their demons, won. This amazing book showed me that this little boy, who knew nothing but death and despair, could nourish his light and become the savior of his home and his friends, even though he had every right to let the void inside him consume him. This book opened my very young and inexperienced eyes to the world around me, to the truth that deep under some people's jovial exteriors there is pain, there is sorrow, there are experiences that make them want to beat walls until their knuckles run red. This book taught me that anyone can hurt, and that it wasn't just me with my own troubles at this young age.

The Graveyard Book compelled me to help these people, get to know them, make them laugh. I was able to connect with Nobody, with his multiple school changes and lack of friends. I could feel his pain with him, and I wanted to be able to change it. Not only for him, but for people around me who may just need something to make them smile, even for a second. Because honestly, all you need sometimes when you are wallowing in sorrow is just a smile. While Nobody chose not to follow his demons, this book also showed me you need people to make you laugh—just like Nobody's friends and adopted graveyard family made him glad to be alive.

In the end this book taught me that not only do I have good and bad inside me, but also that I'm not the only one who feels out of place sometimes. What I learned from *The Graveyard Book* is that everyone needs love, everyone needs kindness, and everyone needs help fighting their inner battles, or else as humans, we all lose in the end.

Diary Entry from an Abuse Victim

Morgan Blankenbecklor

Dear Diary,

I had to stay home once again because of him. I'm covered in bruises, ones that I can't cover up with makeup. I'm sure my cheek is broken from his fist, my eye is swollen shut and it hurts. It hurts so much. My friends always ask me what's wrong; I can't tell them. I can't tell them that my husband beats me when he's had too much to drink or when I have a late shift after work. I'll call him when I have to stay. I just . . . I don't understand. There's no safe place I can go. The shelters are all too far from my home. There are only six shelters in the state that I call home, South Carolina.

My husband has guns in the house, and he doesn't even have a permit to have them. He threatens me with them during our arguments. I know I shouldn't argue with him, it just makes it worse for me later on. I know that he's going to start another argument when he gets home; I started dinner late again. I've thought about hiding his guns, but they are in a safe that he keeps locked. I wish I knew his passcode.

I just finished fixing the table and getting everything ready for dinner. I just heard the door open, but I think it's just my husband coming home. He hasn't come into the kitchen yet, I'm worried, maybe I should go check.

He yelled at me for starting dinner late. He hit me again, now I'm just sitting here watching him drink a beer, his gun is on the table in front of him and im scared of what he's thinking its my fault though I shouldve started dinner earlier. Hes yelling at me again I dont know what to do. He keeps messing with his gun maybe I should run aw—

Domestic abuse is a very big issue in South Carolina. This diary entry is just one example of what could happen to someone. Something much worse could happen if action isn't taken soon. To counteract this abuse, we should have more shelters available. South Carolina has eighteen, according to Sistercare, a Midlands-based organization serving domestic violence survivors. Another way to help is to have stricter gun laws. To buy a gun, according to gun.laws. com, one doesn't need a permit.

Works Cited

Marcotte, Amanda. "South Carolina: Where Men Murder Women and Legislators Don't Care." *Slate*. 20 Aug. 2014.

"South Carolina Gun Laws." Laws. Accessed 12 Oct. 2017.

"South Carolina Ranks No. 1 for Deadly Violence against Women." *Columbia (S.C.) State*, 15 Sept. 2015.

My Experience with Southport

Morgan Blankenbecklor

It seems very cliché, a seventeen-year-old girl saying a Nicholas Sparks book has had the biggest impact on her. But to me, *Safe Haven* has. The book is about a young woman who has an abusive husband who happens to be a cop. She feels the only way out is to run away. Erin, the abuse victim, does. She runs to a place called Southport in North Carolina. She starts her life over as a girl named Katie. She falls in love with a man and his kids; finally she is safe.

Katie gains the protection of her new love, Alex, who happens to be a detective. When Katie's abusive husband comes to Southport to take her back, Alex fights literally to the death to protect her. Kevin, the abusive husband, dies. Katie fully comes to terms that Kevin is gone, and she is safe.

I truly admire Katie's heart and bravery. It takes an extreme amount of courage to do what she did. I also believe that if Katie had not left, she would be dead. So the novel becomes the story of her standing up for herself, as every woman should.

Another reason *Safe Haven* has an impact on me is that I know that town. I know Southport and Wilmington. I know the huge Fourth of July festival they have. I know how the people are always there for one another. That is so important to me, the closeness that the sleepy little town shares. I love to know that someone can come to me for help or that I can go to them. Even though Southport is a small place, it has a lot of meaning to me.

Alex helped Katie, and she helped him and his children. Alex lost his wife, and Katie renewed something in him he thought he lost. His children began to blossom again. I hope that I am able to help someone or something like that. I want to make a difference the way Katie and Alex did.

I have always wanted to help someone or something, like an animal or the environment. I guess it kind of runs in my blood. Both of my parents were nurses, as were both of my grandmothers, and both of my grandfathers were in the military.

I want to be a marine biologist and help sea life, and I want to help people too. I knew this before I read *Safe Haven,* but after reading it, everything in the world just . . . clicked. I want to help people and animals. Just like how Alex and Katie helped each other.

Going Green in South Carolina

Emily Brooke

In the past two decades, attitudes concerning marijuana have shifted dramatically within the United States. With legalization of medical marijuana and
recreational use of the drug becoming more prevalent, the herb has become
acceptable as beneficial and harmless in the eyes of many (Lynch). While
South Carolina is plagued by a variety of potent drugs like methamphetamine,
heroin, and cocaine, well over half of drug-related arrests concern marijuana.
Many states consider marijuana a safe and beneficial medicine and have made
it legally available for patients, yet in our state, simple possession of the herb
can cost a person a huge sum of money and valuable time. In South Carolina,
we should take advantage of the opportunity to regulate the drug and make it
available to consumers for both medical and recreational use.

Cannabis is a naturally grown plant with numerous medical benefits to
the human body. Despite thousands of years of human marijuana use, not one
death has been directly attributed to cannabis; while prescription painkillers
cause thousands of overdose deaths each year, no one has ever experienced
a marijuana overdose (Stuart). The most advanced ancient civilizations of
Egypt, China, Greece, and India all used the herb as a remedy for a variety
of ailments, from inflammation, earache, and edema to anxiety and insomnia
(Hanrahan 1431). Scientists still are unable to find any evidence of harmful side
effects from use of the drug aside from the potential effect of the smoke on the
lungs, and even the lung damage one may receive from his or her marijuana
usage poses less of a risk than does tobacco smoke due to the different amounts
of each substance typically consumed (Conley).

By the early 1990s, thirty-five out of fifty states had legalized medical
marijuana. Roughly twenty-five years have passed, and South Carolina still
has not legalized marijuana, even medical marijuana, nor made any efforts to
decriminalize the drug. The state of South Carolina is lacking the progressive

spirit seen in many other states across the country. In Colorado marijuana was legalized for recreational use at the beginning of 2014. In its first ten months of marijuana legalization, Colorado experienced decreases in crime and traffic accidents, the lowest unemployment rate in six years, and significant economic benefits (Drug Policy Alliance).

One of the most common arguments against marijuana legalization is that more adolescents may try the drug; however, this has not been the case for the first state to legalize the drug for recreational use. One year after Colorado legalized the herb, rates of adolescent usage of cannabis actually decreased. In the state's 2015 biennial Healthy Kids Colorado Survey, only 20 percent of Colorado high school students admitted using pot in the preceding month. This percentage is down from the survey's 2011 data, in which 22 percent of high school students claimed to have used marijuana in the past month. As a result of this newly acquired acceptance of marijuana, the use of the herb decreased among users below the legal age. With strict identification requirements, adolescents are not able to purchase legal marijuana, and many have also lost access to their former drug distributors, whose underground businesses may have fallen through the cracks as they are unable to compete with new legal dispensaries. Not only may adolescents be consuming less marijuana, they are also no longer putting themselves in dangerous situations with potentially dangerous drug dealers who may be selling products laced with harmful substances. Still our state lacks the initiative to legalize marijuana.

In South Carolina fines for simple possession of marijuana can range from $200 to $2,000. This would be equivalent to between one and thirty days in jail. Speeding tickets range from $80–$500 within the state. Speeding kills hundreds of people every day and is a very selfish crime because it puts others in danger ("Ticket Fines"). Smoking cannabis, on the other hand, does not impose a risk to surrounding people, yet the consequences are much more intense. This is a fatal flaw within our judicial system. We have citizens serving time in jail for simple marijuana possession, while those who have injured others by driving recklessly over the speed limit are not arrested.

Cannabis tax earned the state of Colorado more than $135 million in 2015 alone, according to data from that state's department of revenue. Nearly $35 million of this cannabis tax money is being used to help increase the number of health professionals in their public schools, who are educating students on mental health and drug use, among other related health subjects. Our state could use the tax earned from marijuana sales to build better public schools, implement programs like Colorado's medical initiative, and improve our crumbling infrastructure.

The legalization of cannabis products would be a gateway to improving many aspects of our state. Many South Carolinians could benefit greatly from the health benefits of marijuana, both psychological and physiological, as well as the paving of new roads, enhancement of education, and improvement upon public buildings made possible through tax revenue from marijuana sales. We are only holding ourselves back by criminalizing marijuana use and not allowing the benefits of the herb to be embraced by South Carolinians.

Works Cited

Conley, Mikaela. "Marijuana Smoke Not as Damaging as Tobacco, Says Study." ABC News. 10 Jan. 2012. Accessed 29 Oct. 2015.

Drug Policy Alliance. "Status Report: Marijuana Legalization in Colorado." 2015. Accessed 29 Oct. 2015.

Hanrahan, Clare. "Marijuana." *Gale Encyclopedia of Alternative Medicine.* 3rd ed. Detroit: Gale Group, 2009. 1:1430–33. Accessed 29 Oct. 2015.

Lynch, Tamara. "America's Changing Attitude toward Marijuana." MultiBriefs: Exclusive. 21 Aug. 2015. Accessed 29 Oct. 2015.

South Carolina Department of Motor Vehicles. "Ticket Fines and Penalties in South Carolina." N.d. Accessed 29 Oct. 2015.

Stuart, Hunter. "Here's Why Those 'Marijuana Deaths' Don't Change the Debate on Weed." *Huffington Post.* 28 Feb. 2014. Accessed 29 Oct. 2015.

Metamorphosis

Emily Brooke

I always knew there was something different about my way of thinking when compared to my peers. I never saw color, gender, sexuality, or socioeconomic status as important indicators of a person's character. Though written decades ago, Harper Lee's story of the South depicted what I despised about society and ignited a drive in me to do something to continue the progressivism I felt in her novel, *To Kill a Mockingbird.*

I was Scout, the messy little girl who never felt satisfied following the expectations of society. Wearing dresses was not comfortable, and being ladylike felt more like being a puppet in the hands of a misogynistic society that I could never appreciate. The leader of the ring of trouble and curiosity—that was me. Around me life in the South has always continued in its conservative and often discriminative ways, but I've never been one to stay set with how things are. On the contrary, I form strong opinions based upon my own experience and advocate for the truth I find. This is what I see in Scout, and this is who I've been since I was old enough to form myself into such a character.

Approaching adulthood, I've come to the harsh realization that I cannot continue to be Scout, and though I love her, I must let her go and continue growing. I strive now to be Atticus. In Lee's novel Atticus becomes a social pariah for defending a black man accused of raping a white woman. Whether he was innocent or not, the white society in Maycomb, Alabama, did not really care, as his race determined his sentence, and Atticus chose to fix this injustice. Unlike his daughter, Scout, Atticus was a rather quiet man. I've served my term as the free-roaming, curious-minded, outspoken Scout. It's time for me to shut my mouth and continue to open my mind.

I see Atticus as the epitome of a great human being. He taught his children to see everyone equally and defended his truth when others accepted lies taught by southern society. I hope one day my opinions may stay strong but my mouth will learn to stay quiet as I push to become a mature "Atticus" in the southern society in which I live.

Harper Lee's progressivism was far ahead of its time, and she should be applauded for eternity. *To Kill a Mockingbird* is a book in which I see myself; I see the society into which I don't want to conform, and I see the person I want to become. A feminist before the time of feminism, Harper Lee was a literary genius, and her novel has continued to inspire the activist in me for defending truth, equality, and fairness, as well as the force behind my metamorphosis from Scout into the Atticus I hope to find myself to one day be.

Dirty Little Secret

De-Jah Burton

Anguish racks my body as I try to hide my tears. All of this time hiding behind a veil that encumbers people from seeing who I want to be. They judge me based on what they think they know, but if they really knew they wouldn't stay. They would leave me all alone, and let the darkness suffocate me. They would leave me flailing, reaching for a helping hand, but nobody would want to touch my tainted hand. Nobody wants the disease that I have. God forbid somebody be nice to the gay kid. They expect me to cover my face in makeup, date the quarterback of the football team, and then break up. Make sure I wear the nicest clothes, and hang around the right people, go to church every Sunday and be little Miss Perfect. Appear to be behind the crooked line that society has drawn as normal. How dare I try to become myself in a world where everybody is trying to be somebody that they aren't? I just stand in the corner and hide in the shadows. Maybe if I cover my face no one will know. I keep running from the dark to try and get to the light, but deep down I know that it is a worthless fight. I can't change who I am, only make myself better. To learn from my past experiences and become wiser. Only I will never be able to learn from the past if I won't face the present. I'm terrified of what the future holds.

I've always been taught to be who I want to be, but society will never be able to say that with true honesty. When I try to be me I am shut out of the world, because I don't conform to who they want me to be. They judge me for my "dirty little secret" when they all have skeletons in their closets. But I will no longer hide behind the shadows. No longer will I be that girl that becomes what society expects. I will show everyone that I am human too. I will be the sunshine that lights up the sky showing all the imperfections and all the flaws that everyone has. I will be that girl. I will become the girl I once feared becoming.

Deep down I have always been that girl.1 Peter 3:34 says, "Do not let your adorning be external—the braiding of hair and the putting on of gold jewelry, or the clothing you wear—but let your adorning be the hidden person of the heart with the imperishable beauty of a gentle and quiet spirit, which in God's sight is very precious." I am beautiful in and out. My soul is pure, and I know that God loves me for who I am. I don't have to be the beauty queen or the captain of the cheer squad. I just have to be me, and I know that the person I desperately try to hide is the real me. That's me, and who I am is nothing to be ashamed of.

No matter what anybody says, I don't have to have the fancy clothes or date the quarterback. I just have to embrace the beauty that I know I have within me and wear it better than any of the makeup they cake on their faces, better than any of the fancy clothes. Look at me: I am the outcome of having people try to tell you who to be. I am the result of having everybody trying to weave all of their personal beliefs into my personality.

What's on the inside is what defines a person. True beauty lies within those who are willing to show the world who they really are. All the money, the makeup, all the things that make you everything but who you are supposed to be can't take away the truth that we are all human and none of us are alike. Sure, we can all hide behind false virtue and pass judgment on others as if we don't all have dark veils we hide behind, but in the end, we all have to live with our dirt. So when a person openly embraces who they are, it doesn't make them wrong, it makes them brave. Not because they are trying to fight a cause, but because they are willing to show who they are no matter the consequences.

Forever Branded

De-Jah Burton

"Today, class, we will start reading *The Scarlet Letter*."

Those words reverberated through my brain. I remembered the horror stories I had heard from people who had read it before. Would I be able to decipher this? All kinds of questions raced through my mind. Before I even picked up the book, my heart was racing. In my hand I held the book that would forever change my mind-set. In my hand I held the one book that would awaken the reality within me. No more do I have that naive, childlike mentality. I knew life wasn't all sunshine and rainbows, as I had once thought it would be, but I didn't know this as I stared down at this book. The only thing that clouded my mind at that moment was *will I understand?*

I swallowed the lump in my throat and began to read. Suddenly the fear came back. *I am supposed to be able to understand this? I'm only in the tenth grade. I have no earthly idea how to interpret this. I'm not wise enough.* But the more I read, the more my fear dissipated, and I became aware this story was nothing to be afraid of. I read avidly and saw this story had hidden truths everywhere. I saw that everyone was guilty of hypocrisy and judgment. I knew everyone was guilty of judging others as if they themselves had done no wrong. Even I was guilty of this. I witnessed the judgment and the wrongdoing Hester faced because she committed adultery, when in reality everyone in the story was capable of and had committed sin. But in the Massachusetts Bay Colony, a seventeenth-century Puritan society, that concept was not accepted.

The more I read, the more Nathaniel Hawthorne exposed me to the injustices and wrongs of society. We are constantly forcing people to conform to our ideas of perfection or be shut out. Constantly our society looks down on others who refuse to be like us. We openly mock those who have made mistakes as if we haven't made mistakes of our own. The realization that I, too, was like the rest of society caused the regret to rise and overcome me completely. I thought of all the times I had looked down on the kid who was always late, how I judged the girl with all the tattoos, how I judged and talked about the kid who just wanted everyone to love him despite his sexuality. I realized I was guilty of the biggest sin—judging others. Suddenly I understood why the mind can be one's biggest enemy. Every hurtful thing I'd ever done or said raced through my mind. The painful truth pierced my heart and slowly snaked its way to my soul. The darkness I'd tried so desperately to hide suddenly surfaced and enveloped me in a cold embrace.

I read the final chapter of the book. I was ashamed of the actions of those people. I was disgusted that people are like that to this day. I knew that one too many times people had allowed their egos to get in the way of realizing they were wrong. A "man's" pride is a strong thing.

From this story I learned that people are so quick to judge others but don't look at their own situations through the same lens. *The Scarlet Letter* opened my eyes to the reality that although we are well aware that none of us are perfect, we still act as if we are. We are so quick to look at people and label them—whether it's with a fancy embroidered letter or whispers from behind closed doors. We label them as if we have never made mistakes. We judge them as if we have never faced temptation. We judge them as if we aren't human. We judge them as if we can do no wrong, when in reality we can do wrong and we do all the time.

The Scarlet Letter taught me that even people in high places can do something unworthy. I'm not going to stretch the truth and say I don't judge people anymore, because I am well aware that I do. I will say that I am more conscientious of others now, and I'm mindful of my words and actions. I know I wouldn't want to be branded with a scarlet letter, so I do my best to not do that to others.

"Do unto others as you would have others do unto you." Cliché as that saying may be, *The Scarlet Letter* taught that to me.

Everyone has a scarlet letter, whether it's where everyone can see it or it is deep within. Everyone is capable of sin, even if you are trying to prevent it. *The Scarlet Letter* forced reality upon a fifteen-year-old. It opened my eyes to the true nature of people, and it made me see that even though I knew right from wrong, that didn't make me invincible. I was still capable of doing wrong.

Even though my actions may not have differed, my mind-set is more mature, and I am more mature. I can't help but appreciate being exposed to that novel, because it really helped me to grow and mature into a person that I hope people will one day admire.

Improving South Carolina by Improving the Lives of Future Citizens

Alexandra Hurd

To improve the state, we must first improve the people who will someday run this state. The future of South Carolina is dependent on the current youth. While there are many things that influence growth of an individual, the most pressing matter is childhood cancer and the accessibility of treatment to patients despite race, gender, age, and socioeconomic class.

How can we improve someone's life if they are not allowed to live past the age of eight, the average age of death for children with cancer (Kids v. Cancer)? Only 70 percent of white children diagnosed with leukemia in South Carolina will live ten years past diagnosis. As for black children, the rate is even lower, with only 50 percent living ten years past diagnosis (SCDHEC). This difference in percentage can be attributed to a visible problem in South Carolina with the socioeconomic status difference between blacks and whites. This problem should not have an effect on the lives of children. Childhood cancer is equally deadly for both races; the only difference is the ability of parents to pay and dedicate time off for the treatment of their children (Centers for Disease Control Data).

Mortality rates for any disease are higher for those of lower socioeconomic class, regardless of race. Research by Antonosky, Kitagawa, Kaplan, Feldman, Marmot, and Haan shows an inverse relationship between socioeconomic status and mortality. Many attribute this relationship to the higher percentage of blacks in poverty than whites. In "Does Equal Socioeconomic Status in Black and White Men Mean Equal Risk of Mortality?," an article in the *American Journal of Public Health* by Drs. Keil, Sutherland, Knapp, and Tyrole, the authors concluded that those with lower socioeconomic status are at higher risk of mortality regardless of race. They explained that their evaluation of the Charleston Heart Study in 1960 showed "In no instance were Black-White differences in all-cause or coronary disease mortality rates significantly different when socioeconomic status was controlled."

If new drugs for treatment of childhood cancer were developed, the amount of side effects, and subsequently the amount of time in and money spent on treatment, would decrease. The average cost of treatment with chemotherapy is $2,000–4,000 a month (Costhelper). This cost factors in the treatments of side effects of the drug, including anemia, infections, and white blood cell loss. In addition to those side effects, children on chemotherapy often lose hearing and fine motor skills. Many of those side effects require a lifetime of physical, occupational, and speech therapy, realities not factored in to the $2,000–4,000 cost. Chemotherapy is not safe for children and requires frequent hospital stays, which is hard on a lower-income family. My cousin is a cancer research scientist, and his company, FLX Bio, is developing a drug that stimulates the immune system to fight cancer cells. A drug like this would have little to no side effects. If safer, more affordable drugs like this are developed for childhood cancers, more lower-income families will be able to afford them, will not have to pay for treatment of side effects, and will not have to take off work as frequently for their children's treatments.

The funding for childhood cancer research must increase to save the lives of children in all socioeconomic classes. Currently all twelve types of childhood cancer receive only 4 percent of government funding for cancer research. Ninety-five percent of childhood cancer research is provided through foundations like Alex's Lemonade Stand or St. Baldrick's Foundation. Although cancer research funding is provided on the federal level, the citizens of South Carolina can contribute to the 95 percent independent funding. Childhood Cancer Awareness month is in September, and this last September I saw no fundraisers, no awareness ribbons, no signs or anything. On October 3 I already saw pink ribbons on every light post in town. No one even has to clarify what those pink ribbons are for, because everyone already knows.

The easiest way South Carolina can improve the lives of future citizens is by raising awareness about the number one cause of death in those future citizens (South Carolina Cancer Facts and Figures). South Carolina's future leaders need help from the current leaders. Without increasing awareness of this horrible disease, these leaders will continue to be blind to this need. Without action to prevent the deaths of children, these children will never have the opportunity to improve South Carolina.

Inspired by the Fight

Alexandra Hurd

When I was a very young girl, far too young to understand the significance, my parents asked me a question. They pulled up a website with pictures of girls around my age doing all sorts of things like rock climbing, hiking, swimming, and horseback riding, and my parents asked: "Alex, would you like to go to summer camp?" I don't think I really even knew what a summer camp was, but I said yes, and that summer I spent my first two weeks at Camp Merri-Mac in Black Mountain, North Carolina. I've spent ten summers at that camp, and I could write a novel about each person I've met there and how they've changed my life, but today I will only tell the story of one, Olivia Wiggins, and how her mother's book changed my life.

I imagine Olivia Wiggins would be a little unsettled if she knew how many essays and speeches I've written with her name in them. You see, I only really talked to Olivia once. We both have different interests and participated in different activities, but when I went home the summer after I met her, meeting her became the most important thing that ever happened to me. Thanks to Facebook, I discovered Olivia's two-year-old brother was battling cancer.

I don't think Olivia's stepmother, Melissa Wiggins, ever planned on writing a book. I don't think Mrs. Wiggins planned on having her one-year-old son diagnosed with stage-four neuroblastoma, but I strongly believe all things happen for a reason, and I truly hope Mrs. Wiggins knows that her son's diagnosis, and the book she wrote describing her son's battle, turned me into the woman I was designed to be.

Thankful for the Fight is a nonfiction book written by Melissa Wiggins and her husband, Michael, detailing the fight of their son Cannon with childhood cancer. Like many of Cannon's loyal fans, I read this book as it was being written. The Wigginses wrote about their son almost every day and published their writing on Facebook. Their writings opened my eyes to the tragic truth that all children with cancer face. I hate to break it to you, but it's nothing like John Green tried to convince us it is in his novel *The Fault in Our Stars*. Childhood cancer is not glamorous. The Wigginses made sure to convince their readers of that whenever they uploaded a picture of their son. Cannon was pale, angry, emaciated, and covered in blood and vomit with wires and tubes in his arms and nose and on his chest.

I'm sure everyone knows how gruesome treatments of adult cancers are. Almost everyone knows a family member or friend's family member who has undergone it, but let me be blunt. Childhood cancer is a monster. The treatments are even worse.

Today Cannon is four years old. His younger brothers are bigger, taller, stronger, and faster than he. Cannon wears hearing aids and diapers. Because the chemotherapy enlarged, inflamed, and permanently damaged his bowels, he will wear them for life. Cannon is infertile. At age four his treatment made it that he could never have biological children of his own. Cannon goes to speech, physical, and occupational therapy every week. None of these are necessary because of the cancer itself, but because of the treatment that was required.

All of these facts shocked me when I first read them in the early stages of Wiggins's book. They shocked me again when I read *Thankful for the Fight* after it was officially published. These facts shock me today as I write them myself.

These children are forced to have their entire lives changed before their lives have even begun. This book changed me because I learned how this tragedy strikes me and how I was created to do whatever I can to end it. I knew ever since I was a little girl that I wanted to go into a career where I could help children, but through Cannon's story I discovered exactly which career I was made for. In one chapter Wiggins describes Cannon's visit with his occupational therapist and at that moment I knew I was destined to become an occupational therapist myself. Cannon's story has inspired and motivated me, giving me a reason to fight through high school, knowing that if I study hard enough, someday I'll be working with kids just like him.

Growth of a Palmetto

Hali Hutchinson

Bumper stickers, campaign signs, social media reposts,
"We will make the state great again."
Quick opinions, many suggestions, voices for the voiceless,
Improvement for an unnamed problem.

State, *noun,* collaboration of people under government,
Is that all?
No like minds, no passion, no pride of state,
Just criticism.

Criticism, *noun,* expression of judgment,
Evidence of a problem,
Loads of solutions,
No action.

Action less, *noun with adverb,* to not complete an act through process,
Action less state,
No progression, no passion, no pride, loss of unity,
Evidence of issues.

Issues, *noun,* problem open for discussion,
Abundances of issues.
State of action less critics with obvious issues,
Presentation of solution.

Solution, *noun,* proposition to a problem,
State full of suggestions.

Suggestions of improvement are collections of nouns,
Words without a purpose.

Purpose, *noun,* the explanation of an action or existence of an object.
Did colonial South Carolina not have purpose?
Once proactive state excelling with defending beliefs,
Now weak with invisible honor.

Honor, *noun,* describing esteem or respect.
"Smiling Faces, Beautiful Places."
Where is that state?
How should we improve the state of South Carolina?

South Carolina, *noun,* eighth to ratify the Constitution yet first to secede
    from the Union,
Pride and unity brought improvement.
South Carolinians must fight for what they believe in,
Voice your opinion, do not stand for silence.

Silence, *noun,* not something to improve the state of South Carolina.

Mice-Related Inspiration

Hali Hutchinson

John Steinbeck's *Of Mice and Men* is a short book that can cause its readers to rethink daily actions or attitudes. It also gives readers the opportunity to focus on the face value of the words or to absorb the characters' aspirations.

I have a passion for other people. I observe my surroundings and was taught at an early age a simple statement that stuck with me: "Everyone puts his or her pants on one leg at a time." In *Of Mice and Men,* two men in early twentieth-century California move from ranch to ranch to set a new life for themselves, a life they dreamed of. The story revolves around the main character, not the stocky, towering, autistic Lennie but instead the stout George, who plans for a successful future. Lennie aimlessly follows George, and Steinbeck forces the reader to recognize that Lennie is powerfully dependent on George. Upon reading this treasure and realizing Lennie's condition, I realized America as a nation has evolved in special education programs. Though understanding that education was not available to any individual, as George or Lennie in Steinbeck's time, the condition of Lennie's autism still troubled me. The way he was overlooked and mistreated as a human being kept me reading the book with pity for Lennie's heart.

Lennie seemed to be neglected throughout the story because everyone knew he was different. With my heart driven by the feelings of others, I understood that today, people who aren't camouflaged in society because of certain disabilities are beaten mentally. Steinbeck flawlessly illustrates that while Lennie was not as smart as the others, he understood what others in the world around him were doing. People of other proportions, other ethnicities, other religions, other mental capacities are not blind. They are not blind that young people, old people, and all people gaze at them because they are different.

As most kids, I entered high school facing the daunting question: "What are you going to be when you grow up?" I always answered, "a doctor," while other kids lied about their dreams of pursuing careers in professional athletics or aeronautical space engineering. Cluelessly I monotoned the same response to the demanding inquiries. John Steinbeck changed that. I wanted to be a doctor to help people. Steinbeck's creation of Lennie fueled my passion to use the medical field to heal illnesses of my future patients but assure them they are no less than any well individual.

Lennie was different. Lennie was autistic. He was not smart like George. He did not perform as well as Slim, the handy farmhand, when given a task. Lennie was a human. Lennie had a condition. He was not imperfect. He did not need to be disrespected for having a disorder, not in that time period and not in the world today. Lennie was a fictional character John Steinbeck created, a person who, to me, needed attention. Upon reading *Of Mice and Men,* I realized my goal in life is to follow my passion of helping people with special needs, the little bodies of perfection who do not need to be told their conditions define them but need to define their conditions.

"16"

Jaynae Jefferson

I wrote a bucket list when I was 16
Because I didn't know what life means
Or how life seems
Or if I should go by what I see around me?

Why do Black lives matter?
How can a world be so shattered?
Why do all lives matter?
How can a world be so battered?
We're broken up and divided and undecided
But still ignited
When guns go clatter
And then blood splatters
And his name goes viral
And the death story spirals
Was he armed? Was he warned?
Why does that even matter?
It's not 'cause his life shattered or his blood splattered. It's 'cause his hands
    are black and his hands are gone
But His hands here and His hands show no wrong because His hands "care"
    because His hands make the community safer but who has the waiver?
    And why does he have the favor?
When do we get peace—now or later?
I'm tired of being a martyr I'm tired of living in horror.

The confederate flag is down so now does my life matter?
Your heritage, my history . . . when will we solve the mystery?

I live here
You live here
But am I living or am I existing?
We need to be unbroken and undivided and resolved
United and involved
When something bad plasters
And then tears splatter
And our story goes viral
We can't still be rivals
We can all change our fate together
And end hate forever

I wrote a bucket list when I was 16
And I still don't know what life means . . .

A New Way to Grow Up

Jaynae Jefferson

A book that has called me to action is Michelle Tea's *How to Grow Up*. Reading this memoir was a stretch for me, because it basically went against everything I was raised to believe. As a child I was taught there is elementary school, middle school, high school, and college. Up until a certain point in my life, I never knew college was a choice. I never knew it was *my* choice. Later on in middle school I started realizing college was expensive—very expensive—and how was I going to find the money? My parents taught me academics would be my key to my financial burden.

Now here I am in high school, and my English teacher gave the class an assignment to read a book of our own choice for Christmas break. I thought, "Oh wow, a book of choice, no way," so I went to the library and a small book with a woman with wild red hair and tattoos on her chest posing on the cover caught my attention. It was Michelle Tea. I picked up the book and the table of contents was very . . . interesting. So I checked it out, thinking to myself that this book will probably be all over the place and weird. I put it on the table in my room and forgot about it. But one day over winter break I surprisingly got bored, so I found the book and began reading.

Ultimately all I could say was *wow.* I was completely blown away by her life story. This was honestly one of the first times I had read, seen, or even heard of someone not doing life the "right way." I wouldn't say Michelle was a free spirit; I would say she went with the flow of things. She didn't go to college straight out of high school, she didn't become a housewife like others she grew up with during the 1980s. She was an activist and feminist without a distinct plan for her future. In her memoir she tells about the soul-searching journey she went through to finally "grow up." She tells about how she didn't get to that point in her life until she was forty-three years old and that she has no regrets. But she reached her goals, she lived her dream, and she was *happy.*

She lived in broken-down apartments, worked dead-end jobs, but still managed to put her writing aspirations first, leading her to be a highly recognized author and poet. I'd also say she changed a life . . . mine.

Although I still want to go to college and do it the way my parents taught me, I also know I have a choice, and I have to do what will make me happy my way. I feel like I have seen life through someone else's eyes, and I have seen happiness achieved without degrees, connections, or rich parents.

Her memoir is something I will take with me forever. The action it called me to was to put my happiness first.

How Can You Fix It?

Mya' Johnson-Jones

How can you fix a place so corrupt?
A place with many problems and you're
Asking how can that be fixed.
You can't fix South Carolina.
It's a place that just sits there.
South Carolina itself can't be fixed.
South Carolina itself isn't bad.
It's the people within the state.
Funding for schools is low.
Cutting the funds for arts, teachers are
Leaving the school.
Education for learning in schools
Dropping.
Expecting to have a high graduation
Rate.
How can you expect any of that?
Wait . . . you can't.
Taking down a flag that should've
Been taken down years ago.

Holding on to complete ignorance.
Saying no it's my heritage.
You're holding on to anger and
Ignorance that your parents
And grandparents had.
Seeing that and dealing
With people carrying on with

Something that doesn't fully
Click with them.
Do they not realize how
They're just poisoning themselves
With pure hatred?
Can they not see what they're
Making themselves become?
And you're asking them how
To fix it.
A state that has a high
Rate of domestic violence.
Men hitting women.
Women hitting men.
Men abusing children.
Women abusing children.
I thought you were supposed
To love your children.
Am I wrong?
I thought you were supposed
To love your children.
I thought you were supposed
To try and keep your lover
From harm . . . not to give
Them harm.
I guess I'm wrong again.
One of the places with
The highest obesity rate.
People getting bigger by
The day and hour.
Having problems more
And more with health.
Having a risk of dying
Because of their weight.
They know what they're
Eating.
They know what's good
And what's bad for them.
Just because something is
Good, does not mean you

Should eat that all the time.
How can you fix a place where
Racism stayed,
Since day one South Carolina
Has been racist.
As soon as the European
Travelers came upon Native
American soil.
The same place that held
Plantations.
Had slaves that weren't
Seen as people.
They were seen as property.
Judged by the color of their skin.
They were not superior.
Same place that did not
Want blacks and whites in the
Same schools.
The same place with policemen
Killing black males.
Still going through racism today.
Asking how can this be fixed.
This is ridiculous how asking
A question like this, makes
Answering seem simple when
It's not.
Just how asking how can we
Make the world a better place.
The world isn't a bad place. It's
The people living in the world
Who make it seem terrible.
There are good and bad people
In this world.
The world without people,
Is just a planet that revolves
Around the sun, having the
Moon revolve around the earth
And the stars.
Tell me how that's a horrible

Place.
Then you now add people and
Wars, battles, explosions,
Kidnapping, murdering, stealing.
Now everything seems bad.
There are good things in this
World.
They are just overlooked.
There are good people in
This world as well.
Just have to find them too.
Promising that the smallest
Act of kindness and willingness
To help, can make the biggest
Change.
So how can you fix South Carolina?
Taking one step at a time.
Start off small and go to something big.
Try raising money for schools.
Stop cutting out programs that help
Creativity.
Teachers stop leaving schools.
Stay and teach for kids to learn.
Kids themselves!
Can y'all stop being childish and
Let the teachers teach you
Something you might need later
In life?
Don't keep bringing your grandparents' hatred of
    something.
Don't let that affect the way you feel
Too.
Know what's right and
Wrong.
Stop carrying the hate.
Instead of abusing
Someone, how about
Trying to get help.
Get away from

People who hurt you.
Meet someone new
Who won't.
Eat healthy and exercise.
Short and simple.
Know the good foods
From the bad.
Become more healthy.
Get over the fact that
Skin tone isn't the same.
Everyone was made equal.
Different shades of skin
Should not determine
Superiority.

We have plenty of problems.
But let's start with these first.
Let's start by how we can improve
The people.
By improving the people first, we
Will improve the problems we
Have here now.

Being Inspired

Mya' Johnson-Jones

The book *Wake* by Lisa McMann gave me a new perspective on writing and the desire to try and write something of my own—to create a new, different way of writing. I realized how odd things you wouldn't expect to see in a book actually are inside a book. A book's unique structure can make you think more. After reading *Wake*, I know I like writing to make people think.

Wake is about a normal girl who slips into other people's dreams. She soon finds out there is a possibility she could help them in their dreams and make a difference. Even though she knows it will blind her, she continues to help them anyway. Every time she enters the dream and comes back, her vision becomes more or less a blur, and she will become more blind.

I enjoy having lightbulbs pop into my head and want to do that for others. That's what *Wake* did to me, because some of the most out-of-the-ordinary actions happen in that book. Having a person getting sucked into other people's dreams and helping them is something I find intriguing.

When I was inspired to write when I was younger, I would go with what I felt was right—just have the words flow on the paper freely, giving me a sense of tranquility. That's how I felt after reading *Wake.* The words just spoke to me while I read them. The creativity was original and raw. Seeing the distinct characters and how they relate and act toward one another helps create the story and develop the causes and effects that happen in the future when something goes wrong.

Writing poems helps the words flow for me. Making everything smooth and aligned with one another. Giving the readers different feelings and emotions while reading them. Giving someone a purpose to keep reading and look forward to it. If someone is having a bad day, they read to make themselves feel better. Giving words of wisdom to a stranger just from reading what I wrote really inspires me. *Wake,* that one book in particular, gave me a new reason to write. Not just putting any words on a piece of paper, it's about giving a new understanding of what you have written.

Anyone can write a story with a character doing amazing stunts and going through their struggles. Then again, only certain ones can make it come alive and make a difference in what people feel when they are reading.

Instead of forcing words you cannot yourself love, then write what feels right to you. Your words can make a difference. Your words belong and come from you. Your words are you. No one can write like you, because it's your own original creation.

That's how I feel. And that's why reading *Wake* made me begin writing once again.

Renewing Our Reputation, Expanding Our Borders

Eliza Kapeluck

Recently on Twitter, I saw a tweet reading, "I honestly feel bad for you if you weren't raised in South Carolina." With all the turmoil that has been plaguing South Carolina, it struck me as a bit presumptuous to claim it is the best place to be raised. Is this one's actual logic or just the diehard pride southerners are expected to exhibit? As a high school student at a small Baptist school in the lowcountry, I'd say I'm pretty well connected with the "Bo's." I can rattle off the names of said persons who would fight to the broken bone or keyed truck, whichever comes first, to defend South Carolina. Are emotion and nostalgia being confused with what simply is?

For hundreds of years, bad relations between races and social classes have muddled our history. Constantly there are incidents of someone severely disrespecting someone else, and the public is left to wonder if the action stemmed from racial bias or not, thus layering pointless rivalries. Just recently a video of a policeman assaulting a high school student in Columbia went viral on the Internet. I only found out about it when my French friend sent it to me, saying, "Eliza, don't you live in South Carolina?" The state of South Carolina can be improved by a renewed perspective in our relationship with the outside world, benefitting our relationships with each other, as well as with the increasing number of newcomers in our state.

To a news-watching non–South Carolinian, our state may not appear as appealing as we think. The Emanuel 9, the Confederate flag pissing contest, record-breaking floods, cruise ship legal battles—all have defined the common outsider's view of our home. Unfriendly and too often deadly relations between policemen and civilians really don't make for the best place to be raised, seemingly. It may appear as though there has been no change in racial relations in a long time. Sure, many South Carolinians can say they had a great childhood, myself included. But it's clear that a foreigner, an outsider, a non–South Carolinian may have apprehensions. What image does our public track record conjure to someone who doesn't know, for example, the camaraderie of the Clemson-Carolina rivalry? Our state is understood differently by someone who doesn't know the upstate in fall, with the golden leaves populating the foothills, or tubing on Lake Moultrie in the hot summer, or the sight of a crowded coastal sandbar on the first warm weekend of the year.

Charleston, recently, has become a very forward-thinking city, winning praise from countless magazines and media outlets for its historic beauty, elegant nightlife, and trendy food. In 2015 an unsightly amount of negative news coverage plagued the city because of the tragedies that took place here. It will be interesting to see if the rest of the world overlooks them when appraising Charleston in return for a "Top 10 Weekend Vacation" award. Will *Travel + Leisure* overlook the time a police officer shot an unarmed Walter Scott eight times, or when a wisp of hurricane severely flooded the town, making news headlines worldwide? South Carolinians are quick to point out that after such cataclysms, there were great demonstrations of community and willingness to help one's neighbor. It's true of human nature that compassion is shown in moments of disaster. South Carolinians have a pride in their state that can't be shaken.

We must make it known how truly great we are as a state and a people. This dream can be achieved by creating close ties and personal friendships with outside countries and organizations. It's no secret that immigrants, regardless of legal status, carry a stigma they don't deserve. Making world history and foreign language a higher priority in schools will increase an awareness that there *are* other ways to live and that there is a world bigger than our state's 32,020 square miles. Expanding opportunities for high school and college students to make a foreign exchange will create empathy for other cultures, as well as leave lasting positive impressions of South Carolinians on the communities where they studied.

We should capitalize on our positive contributions and strong suits instead of remaining idle in our shortcomings. If we can simply come to terms with the idea of a foreigner having a positive connotation, the horizons of South Carolina will be expanded in terms of education and world awareness.

People Skills

Eliza Kapeluck

Great books create parallels in their readers' lives, even with out-of-context scenarios. Recently, under the recommendation of a teacher/mentor, I read *Americanah,* by Chimamanda Adichie. Although the book is fiction, Adichie uses her own experiences to create the story. A successful Nigerian immigrant works her way up to fall in with the intellectual crowd of Harvard, Yale, and Princeton. What the main character, Ifemelu, has trouble grasping is that no matter how much she achieves, her identity as an African immigrant is always the first thing her peers acknowledge.

Many immigrants change their names to something more "American" to shed some of their foreignness, to level the playing field in a country where one's nationality is as telling as hair color or height. Ifemelu, however, wears her Nigerian name proudly. I remember one dragging Friday night at my hostess job in Charleston, a woman named Daralia, or something similar, came to put her name on the waiting list. It was a name I'd never heard, and I thought she looked Latin American.

"I like your name," I asked. "Where are you from?"

Rather flatly and with no sign of an accent, she replied, "Texas." I noted her lack of amusement at my question but didn't think much of it. Months later, I read in *Americanah* how exasperated Ifemelu—with her nationally recognized blog, numerous degrees from Ivy League schools, and Princeton fellowship—felt when all those accomplishments took second place to her foremost identity as a foreigner. Instantly I regretted having singled out that woman, for making her feel like that restaurant, this land, was more mine than hers, by judging only her skin color and name. I didn't recognize her annoyance at the perky middle-class teenager's erroneous assumption that implied "you don't belong here."

I am careful talking to strangers now so as not to offend them, or worse, make wrongful assumptions at first glance. I try not to make anyone feel unwelcome, whether I'm in my own domain or on the streets of a country not my own. People don't want to be known by their skin color or accent. People want to be known by their personalities or what they are good at. With racism an increasingly present topic, it is ever important to remember how to treat others, especially in first impressions.

The Great Carolina?

Manogna Kolluru

*Often we go about our day, not realizing the problems of the world,
and not a single moment spent, thinking about what we can do to fix it.*

MY VERY WISE FATHER

As citizens of South Carolina, it would seem we would know the state of its well-being, but it seems that we do not. To be honest, I did not know of half the issues stated in this essay until I started to do research for this paper. It is truly a shame how we don't wonder and care about the issues that our own neighborhoods face. South Carolina is a pretty good state overall, but it has a long way to go to reach "perfect."

I never would have thought South Carolina ranked very high on the very worst lists. South Carolina was the third most violent state in the Union in 2012, including crimes against both persons and property. However, the violent crimes don't occur without reason. Eighteen percent of South Carolinians are food insecure. They barely can afford enough to eat each week and are one unpaid sick day away from going to bed hungry. On average in the United States, food insecurity is 15 percent, which means South Carolina is above average, and not in a pleasant way. Also 19 percent of South Carolinians live below the poverty line, nearly one in five, the ninth worst of the fifty states. When you take into account all of the low income of the people, it's not difficult to understand why a lot of people resort to violent crimes. But then again, maybe there is a reason why a lot of people are poor. The reason just might be that more than 16 percent of South Carolinians lack so much as a high school education, the tenth worst performance in the country. All of these issues seem to have a common thread running through them, connecting each problem to another. But how do we come about solving these problems? Is there even a clear-cut solution?

I believe no, there is no clear-cut solution to the problems South Carolina faces.

However, there are numerous steps we can take to improve our economy. One of the steps is to improve public education. Public education may be the reason why there are a lot of violent outbursts in South Carolina along with a very high percentage of poverty. So it seems to me the obvious answer is to improve the quality of public education and ensure that each and every child gets equal and proper education. This can be achieved by creating interest in studies instead of distaste. Also, if teachers gave children more one-on-one teaching instead of assuming that every child learns the same way, research indicates that the child will almost always get better.

At the end of the day, there is no one thing we can do to help a child learn better or prevent crimes, but trying to help goes a long way. Whether it is helping everyone succeed or stopping crimes or even helping every child live up to their maximum potential, it is my personal belief that we can help impact the economy and the lives of many people in a positive way. In conclusion, we can help improve South Carolina by improving the quality of education.

Lessons from *The Kite Runner*

Manogna Kolluru

I was in high school, ninth grade, in a sweaty old gym tired from just running a pacer, when our group's conversation went back and forth from talking about our futures and how much we hated the gym and the teachers who made us do unnecessary things, when one of my friends mentioned that her class was doing a project on a book called *The Kite Runner*. She was only through the first few chapters at that point, but she swore that she hated it. None of us were avid readers back then, and we weren't open to the exotic world of literature.

Weeks later, having already forgotten our conversation, I needed a book for my book report. I suddenly remembered talking about *The Kite Runner* and decided to give it a go. After all, I've never truly hated any book I've read.

While reading the first few chapters, I thought it was going to be a book I wouldn't like. As I kept reading it, I started to feel something—anger, sadness, though it was much stronger than that. The story of Hassan and his unconditional love for his friend Amir left me with a feeling far greater than any words could ever describe. As the pages moved along, I cried, I laughed, I was distraught. Every feeling, from every spectrum, was felt with each flip of a page.

It wasn't until after I finished the book, though, that I really began to understand it. *The Kite Runner* wasn't just a story for entertainment. It was a story to awaken the human inside of us, to show how people on the other side of the world were living. The beautiful world they had known all their lives was just rubble now. Children were dying on the streets, people were living in poverty, food and water were scarce, but that was only the start. The people to blame for all the destruction were none other than the terrorist groups that were feared in the United States of America.

Terrorist groups, like the Taliban and Al-Qaeda, were known in the U.S. for hate crimes against America. Because of them, many Americans treated

Muslims as if they were all terrorists, but little did they know that the Muslims living in those countries like Afghanistan and Iraq were far more affected by the terrorist groups than any other.

Startled by this realization, I began to research life in Middle Eastern countries and learn how greatly they were affected by the terrorist groups. I even asked my world history teacher about it. He told me that the terrorist dictator groups continue to stay in power by shutting down all media, like television, movies, or anything that can give the people in that country the idea that life is not supposed to be filled with poverty and unhappiness. The terrorist groups even prevented all the children from getting an education to limit their knowledge of the world and their current situation.

Khaled Hosseini's *The Kite Runner* helped me realize the extent of the problems people in the Middle East were facing. It made me appreciate the life I was given. It also made me want to help people, in any way I can, who were ruled with such oppression by the extremist groups. I hope one day I can donate money or personally go help the nations suffering from oppression.

This Crystal Is Not a Girl's Best Friend

Alan Lanxton

Imagine a substance that could give you immediate bursts of strength and happiness, and all you have to do to obtain that is put your entire life at stake. That's what methamphetamines can do for you. All you have to do is risk a few minor side effects such as liver damage, kidney damage, lung damage, severe tooth decay, malnutrition, constant disorientation, psychosis, depression, permanent brain damage, permanent damage to your blood vessels, and do not forget the increased risk of stroke. Methamphetamine, better known as "meth," is making its destructive nature present in our state.

In 2007, there were a reported twenty-seven meth labs in South Carolina; in 2012 there were more than three hundred incidents in just seven months, according to www.abcnews4.com. Let that register. If that rate continued, at the end of 2012, South Carolina was averaging forty-three meth lab incidents a month. That is sixteen more per month than 2007 had all year. Those haunting statistics are the reason South Carolina has moved into the top ten list of meth-producing states. Our state is now asking for federal help to contain the production and spread of methamphetamines.

I do not think our neighbors in South Carolina are aware of this situation. I myself was not aware of how pressing this issue is until I took on the task of writing about it here. I picked this issue not only because it was recommended by my teacher but because of personal exposure to the meth crisis here. Sergeant Roger Luther, the overseer of the Spartanburg County Sheriff's Office Meth Team/Narcotics Unit, was gracious enough to email me information on how recent improvements in their strategy is providing them with better results. "My group was responsible for approx. 85–90 labs and well over 400 arrests last year," Luther informed me. That is a reassuring comment about what has become a frightful situation.

In Lyman, which is very close to James F. Byrnes High School in Duncan, you hear people making jokes about using meth and other drugs as comic relief, as if it is no big deal. I'm very disappointed that we have not talked about this epidemic in the classroom setting at school; this is something I would have rather been aware of much sooner. When I shared this information with my peers about how serious this problem is in our state they were appalled at just how drastic the situation is becoming. The television show *Breaking Bad* shows firsthand the results of crystal meth on a person's body and mind, but what I hear people talk about from the show is how the business works. My mother watched the entire series a summer ago. When I asked her about it, she said, "Oh, it definitely focused more on the business of meth rather than the dangers of it on the people." *Breaking Bad* has exposed methamphetamine, but under the light of action and competition in the drug market. The show didn't capitalize on the destructive nature of the drug itself.

Our community also may not be aware of the environmental dangers that meth brings along with all its other deathly circumstances. The chemicals that go into creating meth cause immense pollution to the air, and people who are exposed to the chemicals while they are "cooking" can be considered infected by the absurd amount of deadly toxins. Not only is meth itself a danger to nature, but just about every component used to make it can be detrimental separately. These components include battery acid, drain cleaner, and paint thinner. The Drug Enforcement Administration needs to enforce the proper cleanup and disposal of what is becoming a growing "industry" in our community.

The unfortunate popularity of meth has risen quietly in our community, and as of right now does not show signs of dying down. In 2008 the site www .drugfreeworld.org reported that a whopping 13 million teenagers have tried methamphetamine in the United States. That is a simply awful statistic to have to hear. The termination of meth needs to become a top priority, and the termination needs to be immediate.

Works Cited

Foundation for a Drug-Free World. "Short- and Long-Term Side Effects of Crystal Methamphetamine on the Body." N.d. Accessed 2 Nov. 2015.

Lanxton, Laura. Personal interview. 28 Oct. 2015.

Luther, Roger. Email interview. 2 Nov. 15.

WCIV-TV. "The Meth Epidemic." N.d. Accessed 2 Nov. 2015.

WIS-TV. "Interactive Map: Meth Lab Operations in South Carolina." N.d. Accessed 2 Nov. 2015.

How *Captain Underpants* Decided My Future

Alan Lanxton

My life today has been influenced by so many different elements, and each one has had one thing in common—words. Words are what have put ideas, people, and urges in my head. One influential example I read very early in my life. It was actually a series of several books by Dav Pilkey, all under one title, *Captain Underpants*. Obviously these books are not a hard-hitting exposition on life or anything, but I believe they're one of the things that have inspired me with creativity.

An eight-year-old reading these books is not trying to dissect them for a deeper meaning; that child is reading them because the books speak to the exploding fireworks constantly going off in his or her brain. I pride myself on my fireworks and the blessed ability I have been given to show others those fireworks. This series of books was the first I had ever indulged in. Each and every page reminded me of myself. I had similar thoughts of fighting aliens and talking toilets, and this series made me realize the power words have. As simple as the words in these books may have been, they spoke to me. Books like these, along with miniature theatrical sketches we did in my classes, are what built the groundwork for my love today, acting.

In middle school my growing brain went through a time in which it thought, "You need to be just like them if you want to matter." It was no longer acceptable to run around on the playground pretending to shoot fire from your hands. It no longer made sense to transform into a werewolf in the middle of a conversation. It was no longer safe to be different. My bizarre, nonsensical, crazy fireworks were escaping me. It wasn't until my freshman drama class that I felt safe to embrace my crazy side again. That silly class has guided me to the life I want to live as an actor.

Acting has taught me the power of words as a young adult the same way *Captain Underpants* taught me as a child. To think there is a grown, adult man out there who wrote numerous books about a hypnotized principal who runs around in his tighty whities still brings joy to me.

When I was little the *Captain Underpants* series brought a simpler joy of being able to laugh at this silly and fun book. Now I find joy in it because I know I'm not the only one older than ten who thinks creating stupidity can create an amazing life. Dav Pilkey is right there with me.

The freedom to create is something I full-heartedly hope every child gets the chance to experience. *Captain Underpants* took my freedom to create and showed me it is not simply something that can bring only me joy, but joy to others. No matter what form that creativity comes in, I hope everyone finds the ability to share it.

The Iodine State

Patsy Mejia-Rocha

Ask any student in my chemistry class
"What is iodine?"
And, I'd bet anything, they'll respond
With, "One of them block things on
The Periodic Table, ain't it?"
Ask them to name any event in the
History of South Carolina and one or two
Might say, "That church shooting."
While the rest just stare at you
Awkwardly. These are the students
That struggle in school, the cattle
That never really learned to move with
The herd, so they were left behind.
I have had the privilege of speaking
With one of these students and it
Prodded at my rib cage. Not because
He was unable to sit still for more
Than fifteen minutes but because
I could practically see the potential
Seeping out of his smile.
He sits in front of me in chemistry.
Sometimes he acts as if he doesn't
Care about his education, and sometimes
I start to believe it, until he turns
Around and asks, "Am I doing this right?"
And it reassures me to see the worry in
His eyes. And although he can, impressively,

Throw a football over a long distance,
He cannot convert fractions into percentages.
According to *The Herald* in Rock Hill in 2014, twenty percent of
The students in the state of South Carolina would not
Receive a diploma. We don't need to continue
This vicious cycle of obtaining the same
Low-income jobs our parents have. We
Don't have to ignore the empty desks
Scattered throughout classrooms. We can
Aim further than expectations; we can shatter
The display case labeled "success" and claim
What is rightfully ours. But the fact is, living in a
Small city, dropping out and selling drugs seems
Much more appealing than dragging ourselves
Through four years of high school
To submerge ourselves into office jobs—
If we're lucky, that is. Students need
To see the reality, the colossal realm of
Opportunities and prosperity at our
Fingertips, but no one's really
Wiped the fog off of the mirror for
Us yet.

Pearly Gates

Patsy Mejia-Rocha

I could tell you that the most influential book I've read is a Stephen King book, or perhaps an anthology by Billy Collins (in fact, I wish I could), but the truth lies in the smooth, fragile pages of the Bible. I like to tell myself that I obey the Word out of goodness, but the truth is, I'm scared. I used to have nightmares of Cain and his rock, the giant fish in the sea, and the Devil himself. This same fear led me to read the Bible every night, searching for a reassurance that didn't boast, "Glories await in the Kingdom of God!" Because what if I didn't make it?

I was a "what-if" child. Every meal, car ride, and conversation led to an army fleet of preposterous ideas and scenarios phrased thoughtfully with the innocence of a question mark at the end. Adults would laugh and point out that minds like mine are a gift, all the while my parents would nod and smile as if it didn't bother them that my mouth was never not overflowing with an endless stream of questions.

To me, though, my mind was a sin. I thought so often about the idea of God and the possibilities of other deities that I began to question His existence. I immediately asked for forgiveness. I began to limit my thoughts in hopes that if I crammed my notions into a dark crevice of my mind, He wouldn't even be able to detect them. I would pretend to be someone I wasn't. I was under the false assumption that if I played the role of someone who would stride through the pearly gates easily enough, I would slowly transform into this persona. In reality, though, it only made the situation worse, causing me to slip into years of confusion and insecurity.

Although the Bible sent me spiraling into panic in my childhood, over the years I have learned to interpret chapters and verses, primarily for closure. See, the Bible isn't an ordinary book. You cannot contact the author and demand answers as to why Judas caved in to his greed, or where Noah's ark vanished.

You cannot have your Bible signed by the author Himself, nor can you attend His lectures. Sometimes the most secure option is to read between lines that are not there, and turn away from the glaring truth: you will never have the answers to the questions that seize you by your throat. We will never know, and maybe that is for the best.

The Fallacy of Neglect, Neighbors, and Other Things

Breanna Murrin

In my backyard there is a hill, and on the bottom of that hill is a palmetto tree. My parents had given me one chore my entire life, and that was to tend to our plants. Of course with it being the early days of summer, I was rather lazy in getting my work done, so I hardly paid any attention to that tree. At 6 A.M. I would wake up to turn on the sprinklers before the scorching sun would boil the water on the plants. Around 6:30 A.M. I would turn them off. That was it. That was how I took care of my daily chore. I would, every now and then, check on the rose bushes and much more delicate flowers. However, I never looked at the tree. Trees were supposed to be sturdy.

Days turned into weeks, and weeks turned into months. I continued my cycle of sprinklers and check-ups but continued to neglect the tree. Suddenly one day, I saw it: the tree was dying. From afar one could see the broad, green fans turn into drooping, pitiful things. Upon further inspection, I drew some conclusions. Around the base of the trunk were several weeds and anthills. It was obvious the weeds and ants were aggressive toward objects unlike them, overtaking the vines and small wildflowers that once grew around the tree. The ants had swarmed the grasshoppers and even a few small geckos. The environment that had once promoted healthy and fruitful diversity was gone.

In addition to the horrible conquering was the arid soil. There were no sprinklers by the tree, causing it to be parched. The leaves felt disgustingly dry and appeared unpleasantly brown. The tree stood there towering over the land of death like a citadel of quietus itself. The soil was so dry it had begun to form cracks. There were no nutrients to encourage the tree's development. Without nutrition, nothing can flourish. I watched the ants climb up and down the thick trunk.

The bad had been thriving from the death of the good.

My neighbor, a nosy and typically incompetent fool, was sloppily trimming his hedges near the fence. Looking my direction, he snorted:

"Got a dying tree, do ya now?" I simply replied with a nod.

"Well, missy, if I were you, I'd call the Plant Doctor!"

The Plant Doctor was this old woman in our neighborhood. She, if incentivized, would prescribe a remedy from her book, which was supposedly passed down from generations of people native to this region. I thought that she, too, was foolish like my neighbor, but I did not have much of a choice. I walked down to the Plant Doctor's house with twenty-five bucks in my pants pocket. I rang her doorbell. After a while, a raspy voice slipped from the cracked door:

"What is your problem?"

I explained to her about what had happened to the tree. After a few minutes, which I had presumed was the time she spent thinking, she asked for whatever money I had and for me to slip it through the mail slot of the door. I did what she asked. In return she slipped a creased paper with hardly legible writing instructing me to grind cinnamon, to dust the ground cinnamon over the plant, to sprinkle a few drops of lemon juice, and then to dance around the tree. I saw no scientific basis for this whatsoever. I couldn't believe that she would swindle a kid in such a way. However, I ended up doing the silly thing anyway.

Two weeks later, no improvement occurred. The tree's conditions only grew worse until one day it just fell over. The trunk swung down to the ground while pulling its roots up and out of the dirt. That day, when my parents had returned from work, I told them about the tree. They sighed, a little disappointed that I had failed to perform my one task. The tree was dragged out of the yard and replaced with another palmetto sapling. Unwilling to bungle this second chance, I adequately watered the tree and pulled out the weeds. I also stamped out the anthills and sprayed them with pesticide.

The sapling grew slowly but surely. The diversity returned, and the soil was quenched. It was a stark contrast to a few weeks ago, but all was well.

Holdenification

The Extent to Which a Fictional Character Changed My Perspective on Life

Breanna Murrin

I was in the sixth grade when I first journeyed through the pages of J. D. Salinger's *The Catcher in the Rye.* My father had recommended it to me, and I was absolutely astounded. As I read the details of Holden Caulfield's teenage crisis, I kept thinking to myself, "I can't believe Dad is letting me read a book of such mature content!" It was a book my father had read as a child, and he cherished it, believing that he and Holden were similar in many aspects. Being eleven, I was fascinated with the "colorful" language and variety of characters, including two nuns, a prostitute and pimp, and little children.

I believe the reason why I, as so many others, am captivated by Salinger's book is because of his protagonist, Holden. He is a very relatable character, and readers grow attached to him. We see a part of ourselves when we watch Holden getting kicked out of Pencey Prep and roaming around New York during the holiday season. Holden is a failure in society, despite being born into a privileged family. He fails out of Pencey and frets at the thought of having to discuss this with his parents. We fail many times . . . albeit we hate to admit it.

Holden also suffers from teenage angst. This kid has no idea what he is doing. He goes around and sees how much of a "phony" everybody is. However, he continues to play along with them, ultimately making him a coward. For example, he notices he says, "It's nice to see you" to people he really doesn't enjoy seeing. He adheres to acceptable behavior when expected.

Holden also isn't really sure of his future. As he is walking around New York, he hears a child singing, "If a body catch a body coming through the rye." At that moment, he states all he wants to do in life is save children from metaphorically falling off a cliff into adolescence, to preserve their innocence often lost in adulthood. He, metaphorically, would watch children play ball in a field of rye and catch them if they should come near the cliff.

As the novel progresses, Holden decides he's going to run away and work at a gas station. He imagines a life of isolation, pretending to be deaf and mute so nobody would try to communicate with him. Of course, he doesn't actually run away to fulfill this idea, because in the end, he's not really sure what he wants for his future. And although he is unable to be successful academically at Pencey, his thoughts reveal incredible truths about life, some of which include "People never notice anything" and "Don't tell anybody anything because then you start missing everybody."

Out of curiosity Holden accepts an offer to have a prostitute in his hotel room. However, he soon realizes he isn't ready for sex. He also goes around New York and encounters many fascinating people—some strangers, others old acquaintances. Holden, being alone, chooses what he wants to do, and because of this, he comes to enlightening conclusions: he realizes many people don't care for others and that innocence is possibly one of the best things a child has to offer.

Upon completion of this book the first time (out of several to come later on), I came to a pivotal realization: do what you want to do. Holden is becoming an adult, and he isn't ready for it. Life is hitting him up quickly. The thing is, although it seems he is pointlessly roaming around New York City just to avoid getting yelled at by his parents, he is experiencing something incredible—adolescence, the process we all must experience to achieve adulthood.

Before I read this book, I always did what I was told by others. Now don't get me wrong, I am no ruffian who doesn't obey the law or listen to my teachers' instructions since I read this book! What I am just trying to say is that this book has taught me to do what I want to do. Holden is not a hero. As a matter of fact, he is a coward who only has the ability to speak his opinions in his mind and not to those he is criticizing. However, Holden should be admired, because he took time to inspect and figure himself out. He immerses himself in deep thought and compares himself to the diverse people he meets around the city. Even though Holden seems like a coward for the most part, he knows himself, which many people fail because they are so caught up in trying to be perfect in society's eyes.

In previous years I was focused on impressing others. I never really thought for myself. I just wanted to be accepted, which was especially hard growing up as a military child who moved so often and never actually had time to assimilate. Now I am learning to do what I want, including learning Greek. I want to be an archaeologist, and I decided that's what I enjoy. *Catcher in the Rye* does not fail to deliver on this subject of archaeology. Toward the end of the book, Holden spends a lot of time in a museum. He even shows a kid the way to the mummy exhibit. He admits in his essay to Mr. Spencer that he doesn't know much about ancient Egypt (his essay is only four sentences), but his writing shows that he is fascinated with the process of mummification. He is more mesmerized not by the actual process but how the faces do not rot. Perhaps our protagonist is afraid of losing his own face, not his literal face but who he is and what defines him as an individual.

Have you ever watched *Ferris Bueller's Day Off* ? The eponymous character simply tells us that "Life moves pretty fast. If you don't stop and look around once in a while, you could miss it." The problem with most American youth these days is that most of them don't even know themselves. They are so busy trying to judge others or impress each other that they don't stop and reflect upon themselves. Most teenagers like to live by the motto of "live fast, die young." However, if we do such a thing, will we ever get to know ourselves? And will we be able to say on our deathbeds that we are fully content with no regrets?

Carolina State of Mind

Zyria Rodgers

South Carolina, a state of tradition and devout culture, has ultimately come a long way from its ancestral days. We come from a time of segregation and slavery, as did the majority of the South. We've since grown from that mentally confined era and transformed into what we are today, an overall respectful group of citizens with an intertwined, intricate culture. We've learned to adapt to one another's differences and find a common ground.

However, have we truly learned to do this for other cultures, cultures that don't fit into our knit ground of acceptance? Have we truly adapted to the idea of people living in our hometowns and not accepting our Christian god as a god or understanding the true religion in big Christmas gatherings and sweet tea? In all forms of honest opinion, we have not.

There are always the few open-minded who truly acquiesce to what doesn't fit in our southern melting pots, but in the majority, different cultures are only tolerated, not accepted. We try not to bat an eyelash at obvious differences and pray that no one notices our profound shock or discomfort, but in conversation among our own it's a different story.

From a past experience I've recently witnessed, the only true background information that we possess on cultural differences is stereotypical and bigoted. I know a classmate, a Syrian refugee, who just came to our school. She's the sweetest girl one could ever meet and would never hurt a fly, but her culture is different. Her hair was covered by a hijab, and if asked, her beliefs would be described simply and plainly without any regard to our set-in-stone ways of life. She never harmed anyone, but her ways of life did more damage than realized. As the school year slowly progressed, she never truly blended in, but not by her own choice. Boys often wrapped towels and jackets around their heads, mocking her hijab, and referred to her as "terrorist girl." She was looked at as different, but not a refreshing different; it was a suffocating difference, as if she contained some bloodcurdling disease or contaminants that could possibly infect the school. But she didn't. She never had the disease and never has, but we did. Every moment of allowing and acting upon the discursive prejudice showed that we had the suffocating disease.

So what should we do to improve South Carolina? We as South Carolinians, as citizens, and as human beings, should learn to accept what doesn't mirror what we're used to, what doesn't mirror who we are. There is plenty in this world we do not understand or agree with, but respect is a common virtue we should practice toward those we don't know, just like we practice it toward our elders, our community leaders, and even our friends. Luckily, our common ways of life involve an obligation of respect and courtesy to one another, but our courtesy should extend out of the outskirts of our internalized consistency and normality and into the hands of those who have yet to experience a population quite like South Carolina's.

The Moment I Escaped Death

Zyria Rodgers

It was the middle of the school year, tenth grade. I was going through the motions, back and forth, school and home, home then homework. Fifty minutes for a class, seven a day, and that's all that was there for me. Then one day, one usually boring day brought with it a new book, an English assignment. We were to read a quaint little book, *Tuesdays with Morrie.* Yay. Another book, another hour of my life gone at home, taken away from algebra and biology assessments.

Reluctantly I read, for the sake of my grade and my life, if Mrs. White were to find out how I truly felt. As time progressed, and I studied Mitch Albom's daily life, the motions of work, the back and forth; I began to feel at ease. Clearly we had something in common, and clearly I needed to know what he did about the motions, the back and forth.

Then I met Morrie. I met Morrie as if I were in the room with him, like he was looking directly at me, like I at him. And there we went, Mitch, Morrie, and I into a world of lessons I'd never forget.

Morrie was a free man, not just a civic free or even the type of free we feel when coming home from a long day. He was free from life's motions, one in particular being death. Yes, he was dying, from ALS, each living morsel in his body slowly crumbling. Then there was Mitch, his former student, a middle-aged man in thriving health, yet his life straggled on as if he were dying just the same. Mitch found Morrie again after so many years of his own slow death, ironically as he found out about Morrie's. Meeting again, Mitch spent day after day with Morrie, marveling at his vivacity and aching inside from what was soon to come. The longer Mitch witnessed how his professor and dear friend lived, the more Mitch realized how afraid he's been to stray away from the back and forth of life's demands and actually enjoy the simple things.

When I discovered this story, I was afraid. I was afraid of being free, afraid of being happy, afraid of experiencing what life truly had to offer, what I could offer to a life. I was a robot, a girl who had one fixed agenda in life and that was to succeed in the political, top-notch, professional light of the world. The only goal I had was to climb to the top of this totem pole, a never-ending totem pole, all to count for something. When really I had nothing. As many adults would say, I had my head on straight, but my heart wasn't screwed in tight, so I was stuck with nothing but academic credibility and no passion, no happiness—no freedom.

So when Morrie introduced himself to me, with his cheeky smile and his love for dancing, he introduced a perspective that transformed me. Being the most joyful, optimistic man as the shadow of death crept daily toward him made me realize there's more to life than the motions, the back and forth. I realized I was too young to get caught up in the tangled confusion of adulthood. The totem pole that I was so desperately trying to get to, that I so desperately wanted to climb, wasn't even worth the strenuous effort. Morrie transformed my thought process that screamed for work, paychecks, and success into one that enjoyed the loving faces of family and the warmth of the sun, the laughter of my friends, the energy of youth. Morrie transformed me into a kid again. And for this, I thank him.

A State Left Behind

Hampton Slate

A recent search of the words *violent crime* on the website for my local county newspaper, the *Spartanburg Herald,* left me with an astounding 3,600 results. As of November 2014, South Carolina ranked as the sixth most violent of the fifty states, a horrible and frankly unacceptable label (Meola). Nobody wants to live in a state where assault, rape, robbery, and murder are common or even frequent occurrences, so something needs to be done. There is not really a way to stop people from being violent, but many factors that contribute or lead up to violent crime are also some of the biggest problems in our state. Unemployment and poverty, high school dropout rates, neglected growth or support of cities and towns are where our focus needs to be.

South Carolina has its fair share of gangs and hate groups, with more than 500 gangs with 3,249 members as of 2014 (Municipal Association of South Carolina) and 19 hate groups that are documented (Zahriyeh). These are the obvious contributors to the above average amount of violent crime, but there are other factors causing this state to be overrun with violence as well. As of 2013, the US Census Bureau discovered South Carolina had the ninth-highest poverty rate in America, with 860,000 people living below the poverty threshold. This was 18.6 percent of South Carolinians living in poverty, which had increased in twelve months from 18.3 percent (Ellis). Many people will argue that poverty has no effect on whether a person is violent or not, but the amount of violence in America has consistently gone hand in hand with the amount of poverty.

Many of the more rural areas in our state that are experiencing poverty also have experienced the complete and total neglect of their public schools. Along South Carolina's Interstate 95 is the infamous "Corridor of Shame," where the schools sued the state for receiving inadequate funding and attention because their low property-tax revenues could not compensate. These schools are in horrendous shape. The buildings are falling apart, and the extracurricular activities and fine arts education are the first areas where the cuts come in order to make up the money needed. This only leads to higher dropout rates and the higher likelihood of an insufficient school experience. High school dropouts are much more likely to turn to crime than those who have completed high school (Livingston). It is no coincidence that the towns in this region are the ones with the highest rate of violent crime.

In the less urbanized towns and cities in our state, the poverty and below-average education lead to an increase in violence, therefore hindering the growth of businesses and towns. It is a vicious cycle that these overlooked small towns will never escape without intervention at the state level. This is the reason the state has to take a stand against violent crime; not only does it stem from the underdeveloped lifestyle in these small towns, but violent crime also makes the conditions of these towns even worse.

The violence in South Carolina does not only come from these small, ignored towns, though. Many of the state's larger cities fight a tough battle against violent crime. Spartanburg, the city I call home, is otherwise known as the twenty-first most dangerous city in the nation as of 2015. The government housing surrounding downtown is very rundown and typically known as places dangerous to visit or go near (Neighborhood Scout, "Neighborhood Scout's Most Dangerous Cities"). On average, there are 527 violent crimes each year in the city of Spartanburg. Scary enough, that number does not even include the suburban areas surrounding it—Boiling Springs, Fairforest, Inman, Duncan, Woodruff, Cowpens, and more—which make up the large majority of the county. The violent crime rate in the city of Spartanburg is about 14 violent crimes per 1,000 people annually, a statistic that becomes very unsettling when placed next to the national median of 3.8 per 1,000 (Neighborhood Scout, "Crime Rates").

These are only a few of the statistics that show the shocking amount of violent crime in South Carolina. While the cities of Charleston, Columbia, and Greenville are constantly growing and progressing, they are leaving their neighboring towns and cities fifty years in the past as they try to overcome the largest obstacle holding them back as a community—violent crime. There are many ways South Carolina could be improved as a state, but targeting and stopping violent crime at the source needs to become a priority.

Works Cited

Ellis, Sarah. "South Carolina Poverty Rate Nearly Steady but Still Ranks 9th Highest." *(Columbia, S.C.) State.* 20 Sept. 2014. Accessed 2 Nov. 2015.

Livingston, Ashley. "Report: Dropouts More Likely to Become Criminals." *Las Vegas Sun.* 2 Oct. 2008. Accessed 2 Nov. 2015.

Meola, Andrew. "The Most Violent Crime-Ridden States in America." The Street. 23 Nov. 2014. Accessed 2 Nov. 2015.

Municipal Association of South Carolina. "Gangs in South Carolina." N.d. Accessed 2 Nov. 2015.

Neighborhood Scout. "Crime Rates for Spartanburg, SC." 2015. Accessed 2 Nov. 2015.

Neighborhood Scout. "Neighborhood Scout's Most Dangerous Cities—2015 Top 100 Most Dangerous Cities in the U.S." N.d. Accessed 2 Nov. 2015.

Zahriyeh, Ehab. "South Carolina Has 19 Active Hate Groups, Monitor Says." Al Jazeera America. 19 June 2015. Accessed 2 Nov. 2015.

Feeling Invisible

Hampton Slate

Throughout my short sixteen years of life, I have read numerous books through school, summer reading programs, and just in my free time when I felt the need to dive into the stories someone else has to offer. I have always been an avid reader of fiction, especially when I was younger. An adventurous spirit was something I've always considered myself to have, and I loved to read stories of faraway places and escapades that weren't the slightest bit real. However, the book I really connected to on a deeper level was a different kind of fiction. *Invisible Man* by Ralph Ellison really united me with its main character and inspired me in a different way. While many of my honors English classmates despised this novel, I was the minority, because I reveled in it.

In *Invisible Man,* the main character is different from his peers. He is a young black man from the South with a yearning to make it far in life and to earn the respect of those around him, but everything in the world seems to be pitted against him. Even though this character and I face different challenges and come from different backgrounds, I still feel more connected to him than any other character I have studied. Throughout my adolescence and my high school experience, my dream, much like the unnamed main character in *Invisible Man,* has been the same. This dream is to go far, extremely far, in life and to truly make a difference in the world.

However, much like the main character, I come from a small town in the South, and with a huge, constantly growing world around me, this dream seems almost impossible. I am also unsure of the means I will need to achieve this dream. I don't know what exactly I want to do or how I want to do it, and this is only making me feel more invisible, but I am sure I want to make a lasting difference in the world and be respected for whatever it is I do. This makes me realize why Ellison never names his character: his identity is a mystery because he does not know how to achieve his dreams, making him feel lost in the world. Yet against all odds, he fights through obstacles and even in an odd twist, he somewhat realizes or at least finds some kind of identity in his travels. In my own life I can learn from the mistakes of this character as well as find motivation and guidance by relating to this "invisible" man.

The racism and hatred Ellison's character faces are more extreme than the problems of academic competition, the choice of a career path, and college acceptance that I face. However, this only motivates me more to work hard to find my path in life as I too struggle to figure out my identity and how better to serve this world. This is how I will let my adventurous spirit persist. That is why *Invisible Man* was a pivotal novel in my literary experience and really changed my entire life.

I've realized that sometimes for me, as a sixteen-year-old in high school, it seems much easier to stay underground than to deal with my own complexities and honor my own responsibilities. Although I know what the right thing is to do, it may take sacrifices to do the right thing, which, ultimately, is what makes me want to surface from being the Invisible Man to the Visible Man.

SENIORS

Losing Jake

A South Carolina Problem

Erintrude Wrona

In the seventh grade I moved to South Carolina, and after my first day at Indian Land Middle, in a city too small to be recognized on maps, a boy named Jake squeezed next to me on the overflowing yellow school bus. We talked about algebra, the logic lapses in Rick Riordan's Percy Jackson series, and how we wished we had more buses or fewer students or more funding. We sat together the next day and the day after, and somewhere it became understood that it was us against the world.

We followed each other through the years, through the thin hallways of our middle school then high school, through the side doors out to the trailers we used in place of classrooms, because our school couldn't afford to properly accommodate the city's growing population. But I stopped following him when he became a straight-C student because I thought I was better than he was. While I wrote, studied, and practiced flute, he spent his afternoons wasting time at the local park skateboarding or flirting with girls who weren't me. I was jealous and angry, and I blamed *him* for his failure. I looked at him, jaded, like he let his intelligence slip away and now was the shell of my best friend. I didn't realize he was the victim of a bigger failure, a system constantly losing the minds of children, a school that couldn't care about him. I thought he gave up on himself. I thought he was the disappointment. I thought kids like him were the problem with South Carolina.

I continued believing that until we had French class together in our sophomore year. We sat right beside each other in the back of the room. He folded paper airplanes while the teacher reviewed vocabulary, and even when Monsieur Morrow noticed Jake's lack of attention, he didn't say anything. My

French teacher didn't have to say it. His actions made it clear: to him, Jake's education was a lost cause. He had thirty-two other students to tend to in this one class. He couldn't possibly have the time to care about each student. Jake was just too easy to forget. It was like the foundation was full of holes. Jake was slipping, and frankly, with the understaffed district we lived in, he couldn't help his falling. And nobody tried to catch him.

After tenth grade, I left for a boarding school in a wealthy district, a well-staffed district, a district where I would be held accountable for my grades by my peers and my educators. Nobody would let me actively fail, but I left my best friend behind. And now, Jake is stuck. His mother can't afford to move. He is unable to find the motivation he lost along the way. His teachers can't care about every student in their too-small classrooms with too many students and too little educational amenities. Because he is one of the poor kids. One of those kids who can't afford their intelligence. One of those kids who made a 71 in critical reading on the PSAT in the seventh grade but fell prey to things like an underfunded district, a family trying to make it from meal to meal, teachers who didn't fight for his education. I still think of him in one of those bus seats we shared, torn open and in no hope of repair, every morning and every afternoon. I imagine him in a classroom with a biology teacher who wouldn't notice if he was gone and still can't pronounce his last name.

In the ninth grade I thought South Carolina would be better if we got rid of the kids like Jake, the kids who didn't care about school, who lost their motivation, who were wasting their education. I've changed my mind. The problem with South Carolina is its education systems in low-income areas. We need to stop breeding kids like Jake who lose their drive somewhere along the way. We must redistribute the education funding to improve the chances of students escaping underprivileged areas and making a better life for themselves. We have to create an environment where Jake's third Algebra II teacher can slow down a class of fifteen students, explain the Pythagorean theorem until he understands, until he can look at any right triangle and figure the lengths of the sides. Until he cares again.

The Body's Mechanics

Erintrude Wrona

My sister's heart is the shape made when the knuckles of her two light-skinned fists kiss. My father's true mechanic's heart, full of scrap metal and truck engines, has been running on diesel for fifty-seven years. My brother's heart is caught on the fence of wanting to be a musician and graduating from Montclair State. My stepmother's heart is placed under ultraviolet rays, probed and examined monthly because her heart, vast and gorgeously available, has never been like the rest of ours. Her heart has housed foreign masses that tried to take over. Her heart, the thick bloody muscle, was a train pushing on to Memphis, an unstoppable force, an uncompromising machine.

Until last year I didn't think much about the body's powerhouse. Then one day my little sister found *The Wet Engine* by Brian Doyle on a penny book cart outside of our hometown library, and she thought of me, her book-loving sister. The book examines human existence and the importance of life through the narrative of the father of an eight-year-old boy with a rare heart condition and the doctor who saved the boy's life. After reading the book, I started to notice people's pulses, bumping the rhythm of life at neck, wrist, chest. I noticed every human heart. The matter of which all life flows not like raindrops, but a river of unadulterated humanity. The woman at the grocery store who moves her silver shopping cart an inch to the left to let me slip through. An eight-year-old waiting for his slowpoke brother as they run through the grassy neighborhood park, breathlessly unafraid. I saw the kinds of things people write stories about, the kind of love that opens a heart like a spigot to spray all over the lawn.

I connect with the heart of things. *The Wet Engine* helped me recognize the residual love spread like waves of a rock tossed in a pond when just one good thing is done. The more I consider a whale's vast four chambers, the more I want to save a life. The more I want to be a doctor and take someone's near-dead muscle and pump for them. The more I want to look someone in anxious brown eyes and say the cancer is gone. Without Brian Doyle I would've never been called to a life in medicine.

When I first told my sister about wanting to be a doctor, she took one of my hands in hers. The lemonade-pink walls of her heart, so bright. I could see her then. I sat anxious to hear her reaction. I'll never forget the feeling of her blood rushing, beating through her fingertips into my palm as she told me she always knew. She said since those days on the playground where we'd walk the tightrope of wood lining the woodchip-filled landing, how she'd misplace her feet and fall into my arms. My blonde sister sat there smiling, the X-ray of her chest's anatomy superimposed on her shirt, so full, and sloshing out of her aorta was nothing but love, love, love.

The Confederate Ghost

Jasmine Shabazz

South Carolina still has a lot of work to do to fix racial tensions. This state has a history of seeing minorities as subhuman, and recent events show that that mind-set has not changed. In early 2015 an image surfaced on the Internet of a USC student writing on a whiteboard listing reasons why the university's campus "blows." Listed first was the racial slur used for African Americans. Usage of the "n word" from any race other than African American amplifies the effect of the word. Its usage brings back centuries of abuse, poverty, and discrimination directed toward the black race.

Other cases of racism followed throughout the year. The murder of Walter Scott, an African American in North Charleston, brought to light racism within the police force. Scott's case and death was over a broken brake light. The police officer was charged with murder. Clemson University put its Sigma Alpha Epsilon fraternity on probation for hosting a racially fueled "Cripmas" party. As I write this, on October 27, 2015, I can add the Spring Valley High School incident to the list as well. Police brutality and racism is a problem for minorities, specifically for African Americans. To make South Carolina a better place, its population needs to have a collective change in morals.

The American South is stereotyped for being the home of sweet tea, fried chicken, the Bible Belt, and sadly the most uneducated and racist citizens of America. The Dylann Roof incident in Charleston proves that South Carolina is doing nothing to reverse those stereotypes. The citizens of South Carolina should fight against microaggressions—like the assumption that African Americans are fatherless—that are directed toward minorities by acknowledging and removing any praise of the Confederacy or racist historical figures.

In the summer of 2015, a single woman, Bree Newsome, took the initiative to remove the Confederate flag from the South Carolina statehouse. I believe she had every right to do so, because the flag not only symbolizes racism but also is anti-American. The Confederate flag belonged to a group of states that wanted to secede from America. The Southern pride/heritage that many people claim does not exist. The flag is no more prideful than the fact that the ancestors of southerners were slave owners or slaves. The removal of the Confederate flag symbolized the beginning of racial healing.

Many people fail to realize how the Confederacy ties into current racial issues. Slavery and the Confederacy are the foundation of all racial allegations and events that have ever happened in South Carolina. That self-appointed nation supported the dehumanization of 10.7 million African Americans who endured the brutality of slavery, according to the Gilder Lehrman Institute of American History. The Confederacy did not support the equality and justice America was founded on. Even though the Confederacy didn't last, its values and beliefs were harbored years before its existence and continue to stretch their way into today.

Clemson University's land was once a part of John C. Calhoun's plantation. The university also has a building, Tillman Hall, named after a white supremacist who supported the lynching of African Americans. Renaming buildings honoring racist leaders does not erase history but instead eliminates the recognition of a person who caused great harm to many American citizens. To me, that is the spirit of America, liberty and justice for all.

South Carolina cannot erase its past, nor should the population forget it. The issue is that the past is still praised today. Statues, flags, and buildings honor leaders or soldiers of the Confederacy. This isn't nineteenth-century America anymore. People who are affiliated with the Confederacy should not be honored.

South Carolina has a giant Confederate stain on its back. Though the issue is heavily embedded into the land, there is no reason why South Carolinians should disrespect America by honoring men who enslaved, murdered, and harassed African Americans. President Lincoln believed the seceding states were breaking laws; judges have stated it was an act of treason. I wonder what they would say to the fact that South Carolina is still honoring them.

Representation Matters

Jasmine Shabazz

There were years that went by when I read books filled with white people, and the only person of color I encountered was myself as I reimagined the main characters as me. Five foot three. Size five shoe. Big curly brown hair and a smile that stretched for miles.

Representation matters. It is also why I was shocked to see that Jennifer Lawrence was cast as Katniss Everdeen and why my heart broke in half as Rue (Amandla Stenberg) died in a forest too corrupt for a little girl to be adventuring into. *The Hunger Games* trilogy, a series about a dystopian society—Panem—that plagued its poverty-stricken citizens into death matches, was a revolutionary war cry for my thirteen-year-old self. In a way, I was Rue—the girl whose death sparked a revolution, a symbol of my end and my new beginning.

Representation matters. If not for Rue, who would be the symbol of the upcoming socioeconomic and racial war in America—I mean Panem—a war whose shadows are creeping around the corner? *The Hunger Games* was all too familiar. As I sat last summer in my room, fearful for my life, she came to me in a dream. But she was not this brown-skinned little girl but a boy with a Nerf gun in a park alone, just wanting a friend. His name, Tamir Rice. And Panem, so ignorant and rich, so filled with consumerism, had no idea Tamir died. I mean Rue. I'm sorry, but Panem seems all too familiar with their latest products and clothes, cloaked in a city that could be today's New York City.

"Katniss Everdeen."

"Katniss Everdeen."

"Katniss."

"Everdeen."

When I watched the news last summer, I saw Katniss. She had climbed on top of the flagpole at the South Carolina statehouse. The flag of Panem was in her hand, but the news anchor called her Bree Newsome.

I saw Katniss's little sister not too long ago. President Snow's army had gotten hold of her at some place called Spring Valley. The General grabbed her. Brutally he struck her while he dragged her from the desk.

Representation matters. If not for Suzanne Collins, the world would not be so enabled to fight for change. Amandla Stenberg, who played Rue, faced criticism for being black and cast in the movie. The world finally spoke and said, "No more." Amandla became an activist because of the prejudice she faced. Tamir Rice became a martyr. Bree Newsome became an igniter of the revolution, though the battles were already happening in the capital's districts.

Trayvon Martin. Mike Brown. Sandra Bland. Zach Hammond. I would not remember those names if Suzanne Collins had not written three novels on injustice, approximately three hundred thousand words that represented the future, where poverty slept at each doorstep. If only I knew where to find the Mockingjay, the freedom within the world that was built on corruption.

Representation matters. I have been inspired to take part in this social justice revolution within America. I will dedicate a minimum of thirty-five hours to activism per school semester. Maybe I can help prevent another Rue from being thrown into a war she had no idea was going on in her own backyard.

Letter to a Beaufort Businessman after He Tipped Me a Twenty for Telling Him How Much His Yogurt Cost

Anna Sheppard

Dear Mister Money Bags, if your wallet's hunting
a new brothel to blow off steam, make it the beach sweep,
make it Green Street, make it
somewhere better than your life's work of businesses
devouring shoreline.

I need change, need pennies for my center console,
something to dole out one by one
to the Sonic drive-through window in the hours everything's
99 cents

while I pretend the smell of seagull carcasses on the ride to my house
is just the marsh
melting into itself.

Driving south on the parkway
named for your family, I watched a black woman

throw a fistful of cantaloupe at a cast of hawks
footing her fruit stand.
In a moment they became vultures, retired carnivores
needing a hold-over.

I'm only telling you this because
all that's left now is the scraped knee of her shanty,
beside its grave your sign spelling out
Coming Soon: Apocalypse or maybe just
Walmart Super Center anyway

it used to be empty waterfront. Your nephew
snuck me in there once, freshman year,

we slid our bodies beneath a fence of stars, somewhere
we thought could hide the versions of ourselves
we were still working to quit.

I thought about it as I handed over
your change and right then
you were just

like the rest of us, open-palmed, craving any leftovers
I could scrape from the bottom of your coal mine.

Then your twenty sank in my pocket, heavy,
and my stomach was a warehouse
debted to you all over again.

I'll spend that at your grocery store
and catch your nephew in the produce section,
pretend not to notice while my friends dig up my intestine
with their elbows, rushed whispers snaking
my closed off eardrums, *see, look at him,*
just like the rest of us.

Learning to Know

Finding Change from *A Visit from the Goon Squad*

Anna Sheppard

The summer I turned seventeen, I had eleven books stacked in a pile on my bedroom dresser, a pile that, as some twisted, bookworm version of a "rite of passage," I'd promised myself I'd finish reading before my last year of high school began. Somewhere in that pile was Jennifer Egan's *A Visit from the Goon Squad,* a collection of connected short stories recommended to me by my poetry teacher. The book focuses on two characters, a record producer and his assistant, and the way their lives grow over the years. But to say this book is only about them is an understatement. It focuses on their pasts, their futures, the people they've cared about and who have cared about them. It focuses on redemption, on recovery, on renewal. It asks the question, what is a life? How can we know all that a person has ever been through, the final sum of their selves?

But I knew these characters. I knew them better than some of the people in my own life. I knew Sasha as a young girl struggling to get by in Italy, Sasha a little bit older and working in New York City, Sasha as a mother with two children, married to the boy she loved in college, and I knew him, too. I knew all of them: what they wanted, what they feared, what feared them. I knew how they'd gotten where they'd gotten, and I knew where they wanted to go next.

I became obsessed with the book. I reread it once school started. I found Egan's website, where she discussed her processes for each of the stories, along with the stories that didn't make it in the collection. One, she said, was about a boy who would find interesting people in the city and follow them back to their apartments. This was how she realized the real point of the book, what it was doing: it was following her characters home.

Maybe this is what all good literature does. Maybe the idea that *A Visit from the Goon Squad* is something really unique is one I've constructed in my head. But this didn't stop me from obsessing over the book—forcing it into my friend's hands at a bookstore, mentioning it in college interviews, using a quote from one of its stories in my senior yearbook. It was in this obsessive over-contemplation that I found my final takeaway, the "big impact" that just about anyone who's been affected by a work of art or writing will tell you about. That just because you can't read everyone's story, just because you can't follow them home, it doesn't mean that story isn't there. That even though we've generalized the term *empathy* to fit perfectly onto the cover of a guidance counselor's pamphlet, the importance of practicing it within our art and our writing and within our day-to-day lives is one we can't overlook. That everyone has something unknown to us—unavoidably and irrevocably, no matter how much we want to avoid it, no matter how much easier our lives become when we pretend it isn't there. That it's my job, all of our jobs, not just as writers or artists but as people, to find that something, to remember it even when we don't want to, to always keep in mind that hidden story, that home they can be followed to.

Buttered Biscuits, Cotton Hair, Dirty Jokes, and the Kardashians

Hannah Jane Pearson

Loving South Carolina is like loving hot buttered biscuits
    and loving hot buttered biscuits is like loving Charleston
and loving Charleston is like loving an old iron gate
    and loving an old iron gate is like loving slavery's shackles
and loving slavery's shackles is like loving a dirty joke
    and loving a dirty joke is like loving Lake Hartwell
and loving Lake Hartwell is like loving Miss Joaquin
    and loving Miss Joaquin is like loving Stonewall's beard
and loving Stonewall's beard is like loving that battle flag
    and loving that battle flag is like loving a 1960s textbook
and loving a sixties textbook is like loving my grandma's cotton hair
    and loving her cotton hair is like loving a plantation
and loving a plantation is like loving thick, marble columns
    and loving marble columns is like loving the government
and loving the government is like loving the Kardashians
    and loving the Kardashians is like loving Mark Sanford
and loving Mark Sanford is like loving the Appalachians
    and loving the Appalachians is like loving motion sickness
and loving motion sickness is like loving police brutality
    and loving police brutality is like loving white hoods
and loving white hoods is nothing like loving America
    and loving America is like loving the stars and stripes

and loving the stars and stripes is like loving the thirteen colonies
and among those thirteen colonies, look there,
that's my home, my history, one of those red or white stripes
flapping in a Tuesday breeze.

How Mr. May Made Me a Poet

Hannah Jane Pearson

I've always been distrustful of anyone self-identifying as a poet. Funny how I just said "self-identify," as if there were any other way. Nobody is born a poet. The title isn't inherited, and it can be shed as easily as donned. Some people carry the label around for a while, like a ticket stub in their back pockets, but eventually forget about it or lose it or accidentally obliterate it in the laundry. Others adopt the role as a way of life, as essential to their souls as religion.

For me the classification of poet is something I adopted slowly, gradually, held back by my own fears and lack of confidence. A teacher once told me I write poetry as though I were constantly looking over my shoulder. I'm hesitant. In short, I think I'm stupid. I fear and respect poetry like a deity. I'd like to commit to her fully and passionately. Poetry takes a passion and honesty and reckless refinement I've always felt I lack—and what's more, I have never been a person who could truthfully say that I enjoy reading poetry. That is, until I discovered Jamaal May.

I pulled May's collection *Hum* from the library shelves because the cover art included a crooked robot. Perhaps a heightened way of expressing this would be to say the cover intrigued me intellectually. But no. The cover was simply cool.

Even cooler was what happened when I read the first poem. I didn't hate it. And it wasn't one of those rare poems I find myself somewhat tolerating to the point of, on a good day, *liking* it. May's poem excited me. It demonstrated the kind of writing that punches the air from your chest and gives you a satisfied smile. I read another poem, and again, there it was. No confusion. No superfluous artistry. Just good, crisp writing so exhilarating I wanted it inked upon my skin.

Hum was the first collection of poetry I have ever read in one sitting, the only collection of poetry I have ever reread (more than once). For me Jamaal

May made poetry cool. He made it relatable. But more important, he made me want to do it.

May is a young writer. He allows room for risk, for innovation. The energy propelling his poetry was captivating, and I wanted this energy infused through my words as well. I started allowing myself space to free write—a blank Word document or notebook where I could topple words without fear, without looking over my shoulder. I looked for topics that excited me as clearly as May's excited him.

Hum is filled with poems of race, identity, forgiveness. I wrote of love, fears, my own cultural identity, subjects that make my heart pound. I tried to turn these into words that would pound across the page as well.

Still trying, in fact. Because I am a poet.

"They's a-goin'"

John Sterling Poole

Loretta wasn't a violent woman. She didn't want a gun and saw no need for it. She knew everyone in her neighborhood, and everyone in her neighborhood knew her. Loretta ignored her children's pleas for her to move out of that house. Chester and she had too many memories in that house for her to abandon it. Her children grew up in that house. Countless Christmases, countless Easters, countless Thanksgivings. But Chester was dead now, and the house was more haunting than ever. Every inch of it was another memory for Loretta. Every photograph reminded her of how lonely she was, but she wouldn't move away. She wouldn't live with her children. She would certainly not live with her sister. Irene was too fat and stubborn for Loretta. No, Loretta was going to die in that house like Chester had done, and that was fine by her. Until that day, Loretta would keep on walking home from work.

"Good afternoon, Loretta," Albert called from his porch.

"Good afternoon, Albert," she replied.

"How's things a-goin'?"

"They's a-goin'," she chuckled.

"Yessum, they are."

"And how are you doin'?"

"I'm just fine, enjoyin' the retired life," and he smiled, showing his gapped teeth.

"Sounds mighty nice to me."

"You hear about Connie's grandson?"

"No," and Loretta stopped in her tracks. "What happened?"

"The boy got shot."

"Oh no," she said, putting her hand to her mouth.

"Yessum, he stepped into tha convenient sto' and he stepped out and then sum boy shot 'im."

"Lo' an' bahol,'" and Loretta said a quick prayer for Connie. "Why the boy shoot 'im?"

"That's what's so sad about it 'cause it was all ova some cigrettes and a wallet."

"No," she replied, putting her hand to her heart.

"Yessum, it's one crazy world we live in these days."

"That's fo' sho'. Where's the funeral?"

"Columbia, Toosdy."

"Visitation?"

"Connie ain't seein' no one ri' now. Her daughter fixin' to pick her up day afta tomorrow."

"Lawd have mercy." Loretta sighed. "What happened, Albert?"

"I don't know. Twenty years ago we could walk whereva we wanted without a care in the world, but these days you can't take one step out the door without worryin'. Turn on the local news and there's always some boy got shot or some girl gone missin'."

"Mercy, mercy, mercy."

"Sho' am glad we ain't got to worry 'bout any of that in our neighborhood."

"Thank the lawd for that."

"Yessum."

"Well, I guess I best be gettin' on. You have a nice night, Albert."

"Goodnight, Miss Loretta. When you gon cook me up some of that mean cornbread?" Albert smiled his wicked smile.

"When you show up for Sunday school."

Albert laughed his way back into his house, and Loretta continued on home.

The sun was setting on Bethune, and there was a hint of orange in the trees that let Loretta know the Carolina fall was on its way, which brought the more unforgiving Carolina winter behind it.

She walked past the graffitied walls of the elementary school.

Loretta nodded to the policeman parked on the street and waved at Grace walking her dog on the other side of the street.

Maybe I'll get a dog, Loretta thought. *That'll keep me safe. Lawd knows I'm not gettin' no gun.*

She reached her house and walked to her door. Her feet were aching, and she was about ready for bed. She unclipped her purse to find her keys when she stepped on the glass.

The window by the door was shattered, and most of it was on her porch now. The same porch that she and Chester used to sit on to watch their children play.

She moved toward the door and found it unlocked. Loretta opened it timidly.

On the floor was Chester's portrait, shattered and torn. Loretta put her purse into the chair where Chester always sat and crouched down to grab him. Loretta couldn't see much because she was crying.

"I'm sorry," she whispered to him. "I'm sorry." She thought about Connie's grandson and cried even more.

The police told her that it was a simple breaking and entering, and it wasn't uncommon in the region. They said she might want to install an alarm system or get a concealed weapon, but Loretta couldn't afford an alarm and wouldn't shoot a gun, so instead she continued her usual route. The window was repaired, her television was replaced, but Chester's portrait never looked the same again.

"It's a hard job, son"

John Sterling Poole

"What do you want to be when you grow up, John?" is the question that seems to be the favorite among the geriatrics of my church. How the hell was I supposed to know that at thirteen? I didn't even know what a stick shift was or how the Internet worked. I actually still don't understand the Internet. I've decided it is magic. I still don't know how a stick shift works either, but I certainly know what I will be when I am older.

My father grew up on a farm in the bustling city of Pacolet (more of a mill village than a city) in the upstate of South Carolina. He read every book in his school's library by his junior year and knew that college was where he belonged. To make a long story short, he became a defense attorney, and there hasn't been a day in the past thirty-six years that he does not regret his decision. I asked once why he felt he made a mistake.

"It's a hard job, son," he answered, looking out the window away from me.

"What would you do instead?" I asked, staring at him.

"I don't know. I could've been so much, but I felt that society needed me as a defense attorney."

"Well, you've definitely helped people, right?"

"Absolutely," he said, still staring out the window. "But there are other ways to help people."

I sat back and looked at the floor, processing his words.

"I suppose I could've been a teacher, but the pay is brutal."

I looked up to see him wipe a tear from his face.

Teaching is a hard job, and I admire all teachers very much. I have had brilliant teachers who could've done so much more than teach high schoolers, but they decided to teach because society needed them to.

I always wanted to be rich. I thought I would be a stockbroker or maybe some hotshot politician. Then I read a novel called *Omerta* by Mario Puzo.

The novel was wretched, but it was a pleasant distraction. After I finished it, I wandered around the house to find purpose in my life again, a feeling I'm sure most voracious readers feel when they lack a novel to read. I joined my parents on the porch.

"That book sucked," I said as I plopped down in a chair.

"I'm sorry to hear that," my father replied.

"What else is there to read around the house?" I asked.

"*Catch-22*," my father suggested.

"Already read that."

"Read *The Water Is Wide*," my mother said.

"Who wrote it?"

"Pat Conroy," she said. "It's about his experience teaching on the coast in a really poor school with a bunch of black kids."

There was silence for a bit.

"That sounds like it sucks," I said, laughing and thinking that I was some aficionado of literature.

"Just read the damn book."

So I did.

Not only was the book beautifully written, it broke my sophomore heart. I realized then what my purpose was.

So people ask me, "What do you want to be when you grow up, John?"

"A high school English teacher" is what I tell them.

Then they look at me like I have cancer.

"Don't you want to make any money?"

Pat Conroy didn't care for money; he cared for his students, and I know I have the compassion to slave myself away for my students. I can only hope to have a fraction of the impact Pat Conroy had.

Just a Book Bag

Amairany Aguirre

I paced myself quickly in the grocery store, grabbed all the essential food and put it in the buggy. I counted the price of the items together and summed up the total. Eighty dollars. I scavenged my purse. Only eighty-five dollars. Just enough for this week of groceries.

"Mom, did you get my book bag? You promised you would," Jacob told me. I looked over to the book bags and for a red sticker among the price tags. His innocent eyes watched me, but I knew I had to tell him no. There was no way I would be able to buy him a new book bag, no matter how fallen apart his old one was. Jacob glanced at my purse and saw the zipper open and immediately stopped asking. We got in the car, and I saw the fuel gauge just above empty. I looked over at Jacob to see if he noticed.

"Five dollars," said the cashier after I stopped for gas.

"There you go," I said as I handed her the money.

The rest of the afternoon seemed silent.

"Jacob, come eat. Dinner is ready," I called out. Jacob moped toward the dinner table. "After the hospital bill from your broken arm, I have no extra money for the whole year," I told Jacob, trying to cheer him up.

"Mom, I don't understand how you don't have any money if you work. You always promise to buy me things I need, but you never actually do it."

"Jacob, I have already told you. I have too many expenses to make."

"But Mom, you work."

"But I don't get paid a lot, only minimum wage."

Life-Changing Read

Amairany Aguirre

The book I consider has inspired change in my life is *The House on Mango Street* by Sandra Cisneros. I immediately connected personally to this book because I identified myself with the character Esperanza and her Mexican culture and perspective. I too grew up in a Mexican culture and faced the challenges Esperanza faced throughout the novel, like having a feeling of being trapped in a nonprosperous environment. For example, most of the people I know or grew up with did not attend college or graduate from high school. These people are stuck in low-wage jobs, struggling to get through life without opportunities. The worst part is, like Esperanza, the trend continues when they have kids, and it seems to never end.

Like Esperanza, I also felt like a victim of that type of atmosphere and had a feeling of being trapped in it and never getting out. Like Esperanza, I also felt like I have a responsibility to get out of that situation and be a successful person. Even in situations where you feel trapped, I feel like I have to prove there is always a way out.

This book starts off with Esperanza not appreciating the life she has, and she is constantly complaining about how it could be better. I compared her situation to mine, and it made me realize many times I don't value the simple things in life. For example, Esperanza takes a rice sandwich to school for lunch because her mom says there isn't any other food she can give her. On the other hand, I would have at least a ham and cheese sandwich. This made me realize it's the simplest things in life we should value, because one day it will all be gone. Esperanza's mom is willing to make her a sandwich even though she knows there is little food at home, and she does it all in love, because to her that means more. After reading this, it made me remember all the times my mom made me lunch to bring to school just because I would ask her to. To me it was just an exciting thing to do, but to her it meant a whole lot, because every time she did she made it all with love and joy.

Overall *The House on Mango Street* taught me the true importance of a successful person. Esperanza never forgot the people she grew up with, and she never forgot her identity, which was Mango Street. At that point I understood that just having a career and a family does not mean you as a person have to change—that even if you try to change you can never really change because no matter where you are now, you still remember where you grew up and the people you grew up with. I learned I should never forget the people I grew up with, because thanks to those people, I have become the person I am, and they have taught me the real values in this world, like family, friends, and happiness. Even though Esperanza was not economically set, she always had the essential things she needed.

I also learned I have to respect everyone's differences. Even though many of Esperanza's neighbors were what some people would consider strange, she still loved them. She did not let their differences get in the way of their friendships. That is the most admirable characteristic about Esperanza: she saw people for who they were and did not just judge them on their appearance. She took the opportunity to actually get to know them and made great friends when she did, because she understood the importance of friendship. This made me realize the importance of meeting new people and respecting their personalities even if they are different from us, because identity is what gives every person a story and makes them shine individually.

Ultimately I think this book is very inspirational and motivates people to always believe there is a better future for those who seek it.

The State of Things

Jamie Altman

(Sung to the tune of the "Major-General's Song" from *The Pirates of Penzance* by Arthur Sullivan and W. S. Gilbert)

Oh yes, our infrastructure's shot, haphazard, unrepairable,
Our crime rates are the third most high, which is, in fact, unbearable,
Our unemployment rate is, horrors, up to 8.4 percent,
And we play host to twenty-one hate groups, with violent discontent.

Nineteen percent of all our people live each day in poverty,
Almost as many failed high school—one-sixth—and have no GED,
Our average life expectancy is only in the bottom five,
But somehow good ol' Lindsey Graham wants free healthcare to take a dive.

In short, our state in all aspects falls well short of what we'd expect;
In crime, in education, death, and yes, with each extremist sect.
So if we are to try to fix this broken mess we call a state,
We've got these points to start upon, so let's get fixed, and end the wait.

The infrastructure problem's easy—build more roads, fix roads we've got.
This also helps with unemployment; people use the skills they've brought.
Our criminals, without their guns, will have more trouble breaking laws,
And education funding helps keep children out of crime's great jaws.

The only problem's money, yes—but money is easy to get,
SC has had a surplus since 2000—no, we're not in debt.
Just use the surplus money on these problems! Yes, that would be great,
So we can go ahead and help restore some order to our state.

Down the Alleyway

Jamie Altman

Under a certain time of day
Where neither light nor dark holds sway
There is a tiny quiet place
Tucked deep within an alleyway.

No asphalt flowers claim this space,
where chalk-white arrows mark the place
Of the cooling touch of peppermint winds
Upon the moonbird's upturned face.

Though now the dark street winds and bends,
Where words may be your only friends,
The time soon comes to leave the way
And seek the place where sidewalk ends.

(See *Where the Sidewalk Ends* by Shel Silverstein)

Broken Together

Michelle Barton

I slid into the parking space twenty minutes ago, but I can't force myself to open the door. The radio crackles through the half-blown speaker in the car, but the rough noise hardly registers in my panicked mind. I blink up at the sun, trying to keep the tears from spilling over as I try to gather the courage to walk into my old school. Over the last week it seemed I had turned into a human fountain; I am constantly holding back tears.

Last Wednesday felt like a millennium ago. I felt awful all day and skipped school in favor of throwing up in my own bathroom. My first thought would have been food poisoning, had I not known better. I drove to Walgreens and bought some nausea medicine and a box of pregnancy tests. When I was home again I hid in my bathroom and stared at the box. I have never been so scared in my life. After an eternity of waiting, which was slowly killing me, I finally looked at the little symbol that would determine my fate.

I stared at the stick for quite some time; I truly don't know how long I was there. My mom woke me out of my trance when she knocked on the door. I briefly thought of lying to her, but I couldn't. I slowly opened the door. I can only imagine the dead look in my eyes. I had plans, I had a future, and now it was ruined. My mother wrapped me in a hug and said, "We will be okay." It was the "we" that finally made me break down. My father found us sitting on the bathroom floor crying together. It was our tears that dampened his anger. I could tell he was angry and confused, but he didn't yell, he just walked away. He came back a few hours later, calmer. During those hours my mom finally convinced me to call my boyfriend.

I was scared of his reaction. Mom sat a few feet away to give support, but also was ready to give me privacy if I needed it. Shakily I told him that I was pregnant with his child. He started yelling. He told me it was my fault. He told me I wasn't worthy to be his girlfriend. My mom took the phone from me and hung up. That was the last time I heard from him.

Finally I open the car door and face the brick front of my old high school. As of yesterday, I no longer attend school here. I feel like a failure, dropping out my senior year, but I know I have to. I also know I have to visit my favorite teacher—she's like a second mom. I find my way to Mrs. Christ's classroom. She doesn't have a class this block; she's sitting at her desk going over papers.

"Hi," I say feebly.

She smiles at me and pats the chair beside her. I never imagined I would become so attached to a teacher. She is like family. I sit down and tell her what's happened, and we cry together. After I finish talking, we sit in a heavy silence for a few minutes.

Finally she speaks. "My daughter, Lily, had a baby midway through her senior year. She was so close to graduating, yet she was afraid she wouldn't be able to."

I sit still, stunned. Mrs. Christ always talks of her daughter with pride, and everyone knows she adores her grandson. What if I can be happy too? Do I always have to live in this shame?

Mrs. Christ explained. "She did some research. Teen pregnancy is the number one reason girls drop out of school, and 70 percent of teen moms in high school drop out. She was determined to not let that happen to her, and she decided she wanted to help others like her too. She created a program called Proud Mom, dedicated to people like you. Let me give you her number."

I am once again sitting in my car. I am staring at Lily's number; I have hope.

Assassins and Hope

Michelle Barton

I found this book quite by accident. I had just gotten a Kindle for my fourteenth birthday, and I couldn't wait to fill it with books. I was browsing Amazon when I found *Throne of Glass,* but it would be months before it came out! Luckily Sarah J. Maas wrote prequel novellas that are now collected in *The Assassin's Blade.* These novellas introduced me to a skilled young teenager filled with pride, yet very likeable. Long before Celaena Sardothien began plotting to overthrow the evil king in *Throne of Glass,* she was an assassin. Celaena matured through love and betrayal until she was able to face her greatest fear. Her experiences in *The Assassin's Blade* prepared her to stand up and defeat the evil king. I couldn't put it down.

I read about a strong and willful teenager becoming a woman. I longed to be strong the way Celaena was. Throughout elementary school I moved around a lot, and I never felt accepted. By the time I reached middle school the bullying had stopped, but I still felt out of place. As I read *The Assassin's Blade,* I began to see that Celaena made her own place. She was confident and sassy, never backing down. I began to gain confidence in who I was. As Celaena grew, I grew too.

Sarah Maas entranced me with her work. I never felt I was reading made-up characters. Celaena and Sam had become a vibrant part of my life. I laughed, cried, and worried alongside them. Celaena found herself in a few embarrassing situations when she let her pride get ahead of her reasoning. I always felt like I was in the moment with her, feeling that painful embarrassment too. Many times I would have to put my Kindle down and take a breather, before I was ready to handle the scene.

I watched Celaena and Sam fall for each other. Celaena's walls slowly came down, and I knew when I fell in love, my walls would have to come down also.

Celaena and I use bricks of pride and anger to build walls that keep people and hurt out. Those who love us most will dismantle these walls. Sadly they can't be with us forever.

The novellas open as Sam and Celaena are forced together to complete a mission given to them by their master, Arobynn Hamel. Hamel heads one of two assassin guilds on their continent. Sam and Celaena are both orphans Hamel has taken in and trained. They are expected to pay back the astronomical cost of their training and upbringing.

Celaena and Sam's mission turns into a test of their loyalty to Arobynn Hamel when it is revealed that part of their job is to complete a transaction for hundreds of slaves, whom Hamel plans to sell for a very large profit. They defiantly return to Hamel having freed the slaves, costing him dearly.

After brutally beating them both, he punishes Celaena by sending her to train with the Silent Assassins. In the second novella Celaena trains hard with the Silent Assassins and finds her place within this strange group. Just as she is about to leave, their keep is attacked, betrayed by one of their own. Celaena fights alongside the Silent Assassins. She confronts the betrayer, whom she thought was a friend, and saves the life of the Silent Assassins' leader. The leader has grown to respect Celaena and feels in debt to her. He gives her the money to buy back her freedom from Arobynn Hamel. She finds a way to buy Sam's freedom also.

In the last two novellas Sam and Celaena are trying to find their own way in the world, and they decide to escape the world of assassins. They take one more job. They plan to kill a crime lord who is heavily guarded. Celaena agrees to let Sam go alone to finish the job, but he never comes back. Sam's tortured body is dropped on the steps of Hamel's mansion. Celaena is summoned, and she sees what has been done. Filled with an unquenchable rage, she recklessly makes her way to the crime lord's house. She walks right into a trap. The crime lord captures her and hands her over to the evil king.

I was distraught. I couldn't stop crying as I read. My heart hurt because I was attached to these characters. It was in the face of death that I learned the most from Celaena.

In a show of brutality, the king does not give her a quick death; he sends her to a death camp where her spirit can be broken before she dies. She is slumped against the side of a prison transport cart. She can hear the crack of the whip and the screams of tortured people. She is so close to giving up, but then she remembers. She remembers where she came from and who she is. She remembers what it felt like to be loved by Sam. Celaena slowly and painfully stands up.

Then I read the most beautiful thing I have ever read. "The breeze grew into a wind, and she closed her eyes, letting it sweep away the ashes of that dead world—of that dead girl. And then there was nothing left except something new, something still glowing red from the forging." As I read that sentence, I knew I could always go on. No matter what happened in my life, I will always be strong enough to continue on.

A Lost Privilege

Tavashia Berry

Don't look a gift horse in the mouth.

Adults have told me this time and time again: be thankful for what you have and don't dare complain if something doesn't go your way.

But honestly . . .

I don't think adults are much better than us teenagers. Especially because every now and again a time comes around where they can change their communities, their state, their *country,* and they don't even consider taking it! I'm talking about voting, having the privilege to make your thoughts and voices heard and to elect someone who is able to revolutionize the places around you.

For the whole of my life, I've lived in South Carolina, and complaints about voting are running around more than the candidates themselves. A small campaign ad comes on in a doctor's office that says, "Vote for Charleston Mayor." A man to my right two seats away scoffs and says in a loud whisper, "Like I would vote."

Not "I wouldn't vote for that guy" or "I don't want to vote for him," but "Like I would vote." He's not even considering the idea of voting, let alone the candidates themselves. Here's a chance to select a person that can greatly affect the community, and there's not even an inkling of motivation to do so? I really couldn't believe what I had heard and, at the time, couldn't fathom why someone would not take the opportunity to vote. The reason came to me a few months later.

In a crowded grocery store, I was struggling to decide between following my mom into the frozen food aisle without a jacket or going to the book section to see what was new. The book section won. I crouched in a small corner filled with the latest hardbacks, out of sight of any store workers who might want to herd me out. For a few minutes I read in peace, making sure I didn't damage any pages to the book, when, unexpectedly, I heard something that sounded like a mixture between choking and blowing a nose. Startled, I dropped the novel and spun around in my cramped space to find out what the disgruntled noise was. In a small group near the edge of the aisle were two men and a woman, all about the same age as my mom, mid-forties or so. The noise seemed to be one of the men laughing. The conversation was so loud I couldn't help but overhear it:

Guy 1: "That sure was funny, man. It truly was."

Guy 2: "I wasn't making a joke."

Guy 1: "Heh, it sure sounded like one."

Woman: "Well, joke or no joke, aren't you going to answer the question? I want to know how you feel about this. Really."

Guy 1: "Ya' really wanna know who I'm gunning for in this election? I'll tell you. Nobody and No One, the best people there is."

Guy 2: "That's terrible! Even if none of the candidates strike your fancy you should at least try to compromise and choose someone."

Guy 1: "I would go for the one that doesn't talk out outta the side of their neck, but I forgot they're all politicians!" *garbled, choking laughter*

Woman: "You should expect that in an election of politicians. Your reason for not voting is way beneath why I'm not voting."

Guy 2: "You're not going to vote either?! Why not?"

Woman: "Because it simply doesn't matter. Even if I had someone I wanted to vote for they always end up losing or they make everything worse."

Guy 2: "The objective of voting is to choose a person you believe will make life easier for those in-state. Regardless if they win or lose, at least you tried."

Woman: "I'm not a pessimist or anything. All I'm saying is that my vote doesn't matter. Why waste time doing it?"

That's where the conversation was cut off as my mom shouted for me to come over and help put the groceries on the checkout counter. I got up and did what I was told, but my mind kept wandering back to that conversation.

I believe that in order to improve South Carolina, there should be a movement to get people to vote. To make people believe in their communities and themselves. To make people see that their votes do matter, every single one. The power to change South Carolina lies in the people's hands. They just have to own it.

The Battle of Inspiration

Tavashia Berry

I am a reader. An avid reader. I feel that if someone offered me a million dollars to recall every book I've ever read, then tell me to choose one, I would walk away. It's either that or spontaneously combust. But for this time, I'll risk the possible explosion to lay out a book that has thoroughly inspired me, changed me, and crafted me into who I am. That book is *On Writing: A Memoir of the Craft* by Stephen King.

Now take a few seconds to glance strangely at the author. Yes, he's the creepy guy with all the awards for horror novels. The guy who wrote about a demented clown who ate tiny children, a town driven insane by a mysterious dome, and a time travel action thriller about the assassination of John F. Kennedy.

He is also my biggest rival.

Every single book I've read by Stephen King has made me smile, cry gator tears, or alternate between not sleeping for days and having an unnatural tendency to avoid St. Bernards on the sidewalk. His books also make me incredibly furious. Because they're so *good*. Not only that, but also because they all hide some type of life-changing message in them that is deciphered uniquely by plenty of different people.

Quite honestly I know that most people who want to become authors have this type of burning, motivated, jealous rage against their favorite authors. From Brandon Mull to Holly Black to other famous *New York Times* best-selling authors, I'm surprised they all don't have bright red ears from how many people talk about them. However, I didn't really understand what it was about these authors that motivated them to write the types of books they do.

Until I picked up Stephen King's memoir. Despite the types of books he wrote, Stephen King's memoir wasn't filled with gruesome accidents and wacko villains. Instead it was filled with the instances and memories of his life that made him into the author he is today. When I read *On Writing* I discovered there was one giant similarity between him and me. What does an eighteen-year-old African American girl from South Carolina have in common with a white seventy-something *New York Times* best-selling author?

Inspiration.

Now, I don't inspire people. At least I don't think I do. But Stephen King has inspired millions of people with his writings and movie adaptions and just being who he is. That's an admirable trait to have, especially in writing. And it makes me insanely jealous. I don't want to be rich, have a million cars, or invent flying smartphones. I want to inspire people, to give them the same drive I get when I read novels by inspiring authors. *On Writing* has sparked that passion of mine with its tips on prose and techniques and turned it from a burning fire into a nuclear explosion of motivation. If Stephen King can inspire people, why can't I?

This drive has molded me into who I am today, someone who wants to leave her mark and inspire others to do the same. Someone who is not in it for the money (but that wouldn't hurt), but is in it to drag other people into it. "It" being writing, of course. I feel that writing will be my mark on the world and how I will spread inspiration to those who read.

So look out, King and Mull and Black, there's someone else who wants to be a leader. An inspiration. That's me.

The Box That Hinders Us

Mallory Clamp

A few years ago, I had the opportunity to work at a camp for children with congenital heart disease and was able to make a diverse set of friends from all over the United States. One day, when one of my conversations turned to politics, my friend was surprised to learn that I, being from South Carolina, did not hold a certain opinion about a specific hot button topic. She thought that where I grew up should cause me to think in one direction. While this reaction can be attributed to youthful ignorance on the part of my friend, it still struck me as odd. Why was I forced into a style of thinking based solely upon the region from which I originated? Shouldn't I have the ability to choose my own opinions, free from regional influences?

These questions continued to arise and opened my eyes to the hindrance that such ignorance can be to people of South Carolina. I understand that regional stereotypes are inevitable, but they become detrimental when ideas that originate in South Carolina are condemned because they are thought to be "overly pious" and too "conservative." This opinion becomes harmful when someone like me goes into the engineering field, and my ideas are not considered relevant because surely a woman from the South could not want to be anything other than a stay-at-home trophy wife? Or when someone like my father is thought to be less well read or informed because he carries a strong southern accent. Daily this stereotype hinders the advancement of South Carolinians in minor ways.

I want to challenge these misconceptions that southern women cannot be anything other than housewives, or that a southern accent makes you an unintelligent "redneck." I know I grew up in as forward-thinking of a state as any other. My town's motto is "No room for racism," and every year we celebrate the Friendship Nine and their contribution to our state. I have seen gay marriage legalized and steps toward equality for all. I have seen the Confederate flag removed due to the outcries of the people. I know that jobs are abundant, people are content, and our state continuously moves forward and adapts to the changing social atmosphere. I witnessed firsthand the strength of our state through the overwhelming urge to help the flood victims in Columbia. Citizens wanted to help people they had never met, solely because they shared the privilege of living in South Carolina. However, a person from New York only sees the extreme cases of racism, violence, and rigidness that the media shows.

This summer, the average American only saw the racism associated with the shootings in Charleston. They did not see the community's outpouring of support to the victims, and the peaceful reactions of our state. They still see the image of the "Old South," which was repeatedly taught to them in textbooks growing up. Most just see the "icons" of the South, such as Honey Boo Boo, and assume everyone in the South is similar to these stars. To improve our already great state, I would call for the continued attempt to alter this stereotype.

To begin to reverse the years of stereotypes that plague our state, we should encourage media to share examples of how our state actually is by showing the everyday acts of kindness, generosity, and inclusiveness that we are privy to as citizens. Another step to altering this opinion would be to promote events to encourage youth involvement in politics. A lot of my peers choose to accept their parents' opinions as fact. While these opinions may have nothing wrong with them, I believe the state should encourage youth to think for themselves and develop their own opinions. This would allow South Carolina to display its strong education system, which should be recognized nationally.

I want my children to be able to go to any place in the world and have their acquaintances recognize what we already understand: South Carolina is moving forward and is a great place to be. Everyone has a box they are thought to conform to; South Carolina's box has for too long been plagued by the opinion that we are unintelligent, rigid good ol' boys. Our box should not limit us; rather upon closer inspection, it should show our limitlessness, greatness, and pride.

Help-ing Me to Love Reading

Mallory Clamp

I grew up an avid reader. When I say avid, I'm not just talking about enjoying the occasional novel. I mean that while other children were experimenting with their gaming consoles or their "high tech" new flip phones, I was in my room impatiently awaiting the next book from my favorite series. I was the child who requested a trip to the bookstore before a trip to the zoo. I was, and am still, a self-proclaimed nerd. I understand this is not unique; many people love to read. My literary life story is unique, however, because I lost my passion for reading. Somewhere along the way, I forgot my first love.

I was probably fourteen years old. The "cool" thing to be doing was going out with boys (in chaperoned groups, of course) and sleeping over with girl-friends. My English classes were beginning to introduce important novels such as *To Kill a Mockingbird* and *Wuthering Heights*. School was getting tougher, and the overwhelming sentiment among students was that reading was not fun and that the books we were reading in class were boring. I fell prey to this idea and stopped reading for fun. I attribute this trend to middle school insecurity, but also to the fact that reading was no longer for my personal entertainment. It was for learning . . . which frankly bored me. So from fourteen to eighteen, I stopped reading for the sake of recreation. Tragic, right?

Recently, however, I began to realize how much my life is about to change, with college and the "real world" quickly becoming my reality. Soon after this epiphany, some internal inkling moved me to pick up my old favorite pastime. In the winter of my senior year, I opened a book called *The Help* by Kathryn Stockett and was reintroduced to my first love.

The Help essentially is commentary on the social atmosphere of the South in the 1960s. Although I was obviously not around during this time, I connected with this book on a level deeper than I knew was possible. I filled the coldest days of 2016 pursuing the story of Aibileen, Skeeter, and Mae Mobley and was transported into a humid, 1960s Mississippi summer. My connection to this book lay in the fact that, like the protagonist, my grandmother was raised by an African American. I firsthand have seen the unique connection between a white child and a surrogate mother of another race and how, defying all racial barriers, love could be fostered. Stories have been passed down about how my grandmother grew to love her maid, despite the racial barriers of the time.

On another level, I connected with the story because of a character named Skeeter, a gangly southern girl on the precipice of choosing her life's path. Skeeter chose to be different and become a New York editor during a time when women were supposed to stay at home and cook their husbands' dinners . . . and love it. Like Skeeter, I am on the verge of determining who I will be in this world. Her bold decision to go against the norms of society encourages me to make decisions that are true to my desires.

Growing up in the South, I have been made aware of the unspoken sentiment that it is all right for a woman to sacrifice her talents to be a good wife or mother. While I cannot begin to explain the amount of respect and awe I have for stay-at-home moms and the incredible job they accomplish on a daily basis, I also believe many women choose to sacrifice their talents against their true desires, which is really a shame. Skeeter's character inspires me to be a woman who is not afraid to stand out in a crowd. In addition to her effect on me, her decision to ignore the racial barriers of the 1960s is influential universally and continue to add to modern discussions on equality.

My personal connections to this book have helped move me to action. They have changed the way I see the world. No longer are all relationships simple and one-sided. Because of this book, I can see the complexities in how people interact. I began to understand how standing up for a cause is far more important, and more fulfilling, than living a life with no substance. No longer do I sit idly by and complain about issues; instead I have taken an interest in making concrete change. This year I helped host a Youth Key Influencers session. Rock Hill City Council hosted a similar session earlier in the year for adults from around the city, and I helped to host a similar meeting for youth. We invited teens of every background to downtown Rock Hill to communicate their hopes for the future. Alongside the mayor of Rock Hill, I planned a dinner in which our youth could voice their opinions. I was amazed by the productive suggestions our youth had. Their ideas were creative, unique, and reflected their impressive capabilities. After we gathered and analyzed the results of this meeting, I presented a PowerPoint to city council members. Now many of these ideas are being discussed, and some are in the process of being implemented across the city. Such ideas include fascinating solutions to parking problems and new cultural events to hold in our city. Having youth involved in making change is invaluable. This book influenced me to facilitate an outlet for other youth to take a stand, just like Skeeter and so many other real-life women of the 1960s.

From *The Help,* I learned to go passionately in the direction of my choosing. From Aibileen, I learned about how total love can be. Even though Aibileen herself was mistreated, her love for her white children never faltered. The author's use of point of view, showing the mind-sets of numerous characters, allowed me to have an authentic look into the lives of women that otherwise, I may never have seen. *The Help,* in my humble opinion, will be part of the literary canon for future generations to discuss.

More important than any of these lessons is the fact that *The Help* re-ignited my love for reading. No longer is it a burden associated with boring English classes. Reading is my reprieve. It gives me knowledge and experience from people I have never met. For this reason alone, *The Help* will forever be one of the most influential books I have ever read, more than *The Kite Runner, The Jungle,* and *Heart of Darkness.*

Many people are never saved from being that misguided middle school student who decided reading was lame. This book saved a young, geeky Mallory Clamp from a lifetime without her first love. For this reason, I, much like the women from this novel, will be eternally indebted to *The Help.*

New Car, New Rules, Same Old State

Brandi Cunningham

"If I give you this car, there's rules that's gonna come with it. If you get a speeding ticket, it's mine. If I find out you've been driving it like you ain't got no sense, it's mine. And if I find out you've been driving around black boys in here, it's really mine. You understand me?"

"Yes sir," I say looking into my grandfather's face. He hands over the keys to my brand-new car, gives me a kiss on my cheek, and tells me to be careful on my way home. If only he knew I'm not going home.

I drive over to my boyfriend André's house. I honk the horn, and he comes out.

"This really yours?" he asks in excitement.

"Yep, all mine," I say.

He hops into the passenger seat, and I drive him around the block. When we get back, we go into his living room and watch the news with his aunt. On the television we see a group of people at the statehouse screaming, "Take down the flag!" and "The flag comes down today!"

"All that's wrong with this world and this what people worryin' 'bout?" That's what André's aunt says. He and I decide to walk outside. We sit down on the front steps of his house.

"People these days, worryin' 'bout racism," André muttered, shaking his head. "Everybody thinks someone owes them somethin' for what their ancestors were put through. Glad nobody says nothin' to me."

"No, they don't say nothin' *to* you, just behind ya back. Every time we go out, people give us disgusted looks. Every time you hold my hand or gimme a kiss on my cheek, somebody gotta roll their eyes or mutter under their breath, 'That's a sin,' as if we can't hear it. But we do. We always do. And I'm sick of it. I'm sick of them thinkin' that I ain't gonna hear them or that I don't know what they think of me."

"Katie, you knew when we started dating that we were gonna have to deal with this every day. We've been dealin' with it for years now. You should be used to it."

"I'm not gonna get used to it. I shouldn't *have* to get used to it. It's something that's always gonna bother me," I say. "Do you know what my grandpa told me before I left? 'You better not let no black boys in here with you. If you do, this car is gonna be mine.' My parents love you, but he would hate you! That's why I've been keeping our relationship a secret for all these years! He won't approve of me and you! He doesn't want me with a black guy. He doesn't think any of them will ever be good enough for me. To him you're just gonna be another black boy tryin' to use a white girl."

"The rest of your family loves me. Maybe if he sees the way I treat you, he'll love me too."

"No, André. He's still stuck on the past. Just like all those people we saw on TV. They're stuck tryin' to make problems by worryin' 'bout things that don't and won't make a difference in anything."

"Well, not everyone is blessed with the common sense we got, baby girl," he says, leaning in to give me a kiss on the forehead. "Maybe someday people will realize there's bigger problems in the world than black folks and white folks bein' together, or some raggedy flag flyin' over the statehouse. Till then, all we can do is pray 'bout it."

I give him a kiss and leave, driving in my new car that my grandpa doesn't want him riding in. I think about the conversation André and I had, and I begin to do what he told me to do, what I've been doing for all these years I've been with him. I begin to pray. I pray not only for me and André, but also for every other person in the state of South Carolina. Maybe someday people will stop seeing the world as "black and white," and they'll begin seeing it for what it really is. Maybe one day I'll be able to hold my boyfriend's hand proudly and not have to worry about the disturbed looks or the whispers, because maybe, just maybe, they won't exist.

Losing Faith and Finding It Again

Brandi Cunningham

Throughout life everyone learns lessons, whether it's from parents, friends, or even celebrities or novels. One book that has highly inspired change in my life is *Night* by Elie Wiesel.

In just about any history class one takes, the Holocaust is talked about. When most people think about the Holocaust, they think about Jews, Hitler, torture, death, and genocide, something that Elie often talks about in *Night*. He goes into large detail about what his life was like before the terrible incidents and goes into even larger detail about what his life was like during the Holocaust. One thing that makes me love his book so much is that he holds back nothing. The whole book is both so heartbreaking and inspiring. When Elie writes about his life before the Holocaust, he speaks a lot about his faith and how it was a tremendous part of his life. However, he later goes on to describe how he eventually lost his faith because he could not understand how God would allow something as terrible as the Holocaust to happen.

One thing that has always been very important to me is my faith, so when I first read the book, I was confused about how someone could go from having such a strong faith to having no faith at all. However, the second time I read it, I put myself in Elie's shoes and was able to see how one could lose their faith when put in a situation as terrible as his.

One of the things that inspires me so much about this book is that even though Elie does lose his faith, he eventually gains it back. At the end, when Elie writes about when he and all of the other victims were "free at last," he goes on to state that "not one of (them) thought about revenge." Elie was separated from his mother and sister, witnessed his father die at the hands of the Germans, and was even forced to watch young children be burned. Yet he, along with the others, never once thought of revenge, proving they were much stronger than the entire German army.

When I put myself in Elie's shoes the second time I read the book, it was difficult for me to see how he, along with everyone, could not want to get revenge. Then I realized . . . everything that could possibly be taken away from them was, such as their homes, their loved ones, and friends, even their faith in God. There was no point in getting revenge, because the most important thing that was taken from them, their families, was irreplaceable. Elie eventually got a home and was able to regain his faith in God, but he never got his family back. The ending of the book is so powerful and inspirational and really makes one think about their lives and the decisions they make, even me.

I am inspired by Elie to never hold grudges and to never lose my faith in God. Even though he lost his faith, he got it back, proving that God is always with us and will forever love his children, even when we may turn against him. Now, whenever I am going through difficult times in my life, I think of Elie and all he was forced to go through. I know that if Elie could be strong and brave through the worst chapter of his life, then I can be in mine as well—because God will never give anyone more than they can handle.

They Blocked Paradise and Put Up a Billboard

Christian Eitel

They line the roadways as you make your commute each day. They yell at you about the Powerball, what is two exits ahead on the left, and why you need to turn in more ways than one. More warn you about your ex-wife and want to help you out with DUI representation. Some are in disrepair, and some are just old. And appearing on your right is the occasional, sadly comforting reminder that the ER wait time is just "5 minutes." They are billboards—the great visual pollution that now seems more natural than the trees on the sides of our state roadways and may in fact outnumber the timber.

Billboards trace their origins to the 1830s, when artist Jared Bell promoted a circus on some primitive billboards in New York, according to the Outdoor Advertising Association of America. In the United Kingdom, billboards are known as "hoardings." Hoard is exactly what they do. They hoard the skies and are a constant reminder of the maladies of materialism. South Carolina should move to reduce the number of billboards in the state.

The concept of complete billboard eradication has an established precedent in other states across the country. Billboards currently are illegal in four states: Hawaii, Alaska, Vermont, and Maine, listed in the order in which the bans were enacted. Passing legislation to ban or at least lessen the number of billboards would be an innovative action in this section of the country, despite being against the grain.

South Carolina's roads are in notoriously bad shape, and billboards do nothing to parry this problem. Funding for roads in South Carolina comes from the C Fund Law, a gas tax (12–28–2740), according to the South Carolina Code of Laws. Removing billboards would not exacerbate the poor quality of roads in any way. The direct profits from billboards go to the private owners of the land on which the signs stand.

Restricting billboards on private property will be vehemently opposed by vendors who directly profit from their sales. This is a warranted criticism: taking away such a liberty could be considered an overreach of governmental intervention. Therefore special incentives must be awarded to those who yield to the provisional law. A possible solution could be annual tax breaks at a graduated rate for participating adherents or a reduced property tax for those with property adjacent to the road. Since the removal and reduction of billboards could lead to positive stimulation in economic productivity of the state both directly and indirectly through increased tourism, the citizens who adhere to the curtailment of their previous business must be sufficiently rewarded.

Perhaps the Five Man Electrical Band said it best: *Sign, sign, everywhere a sign, blockin' out the scenery, breakin' my mind, do this, don't do that, can't you read the sign?*

The opportunity for unobstructed views of changing autumn foliage, rolling foothills, and sweeping fields throughout the state would be a natural pleasure not fully achieved in years. South Carolina is a truly beautiful place. Sure the calendar covers of the Atlantic coast and Blue Ridge peaks are amazing, but the country roads and forests are no slouches in the aesthetic department. "Call 1-800-849-SINK" cannot compete with a sun-splashed afternoon in April or a crisp October Saturday in our state. When the billboards come down, there will be more smiling faces because we will be able to see more beautiful places.

Works Cited

Five Man Electrical Band. "Signs." YouTube. Accessed 1 Nov. 2015.

"History of OOH." Outdoor Advertising Association of America, Inc. N.d. Accessed 29 Oct. 2015.

ILSR Admin. "Billboard Bans and Controls." Institute for Local Self-Reliance. N.d. 9 Jan. 2009. Accessed 2 Nov. 2015.

South Carolina Legislature. Code of Laws. Columbia, 2004.

Which Tree to Be

Christian Eitel

What book called me to action? Yikes, that's a tough question. I have learned from many books, but they changed me through the flow of life, not in a conscious turn. One book that called me to action never left my thoughts. It cultivated reexamination and creativity. It did not change my point of view but instead added an additional one. Jon Krakauer wrote *Into the Wild* about Chris McCandless, a boy who understood himself more than anyone would ever allow.

Chris had everything going for him—a bright future, as many would say. An Emory double major in history and anthropology and a life ahead of success and achievement. Chris lived his life of success and achievement, just not in the way others measured it.

How can you decide what measurement to use to determine the best tree? One man said, "It is the tallest tree of course: the one that towers above the forest. The one that is high and mighty."

"No," said the second man. "The best tree is the one that casts the most shade. For a tree that rises above the others without benefiting those on the ground is selfish and useless while appearing important."

"You are both wrong," said a third. "The tree with the greenest leaves, which is a spectacle for all to gaze upon, is the best tree. For while benefiting some, the tree that casts the most shade hinders the growth of others. A tree should be measured by its beauty."

Chris McCandless died alone in Alaska—a tramp, homeless and starving. That was how he wanted it. He ventured on journeys not to find himself but to be himself. He was not searching but discovering.

Chris's parents would see that the first man was correct. The best tree is the tallest one, but Chris had thrown it away. They would agree with the second man as well. Chris was not helping others. He left his life to become a tramp and explore the West for himself. Then they would hear the third man speak and concede to him as well. Chris's direction was superficial. It was capricious and vain. Though everyone who met Chris loved him, he also caused them grand pain, because he did not exist as they wanted him to. Chris was the tree he wanted to be. So much of the time, we aspire to be the tree others think we should be. This book reminded me to incontrovertibly grow toward further understanding, development, and purpose.

Loved by Everyone

Alexis Etheredge

A young girl walks into a daycare center for her first day. Clutching her mother's soft hand, the shy three-year-old looks at the building around her. The other children are already in classrooms. She would've been earlier if her mother didn't take her time getting there. The truth is, her mother was terrified of taking her and had even made plans on just sending her to her grandmother's instead. She had even started to turn on to their street before she realized what she was doing. The mother wasn't upset that she had to leave her child; she had done it before, but never with people who didn't know her situation.

Her daughter was special, that much was obvious, just not in the way most people would think. She wasn't mentally or physically handicapped, though people acted as though her beautiful baby girl was the source of sin. Her daughter wouldn't understand why people didn't like her or the other kids didn't want to play with her. She thought she was like everyone else. She wasn't taught to judge, but everyone around her was. To her, her momma and daddy were just like everyone else's. She didn't see the big difference everyone else saw, but to those around her, her mother and father were freaks of nature.

It wasn't heard of in many small South Carolina towns for people to be in an interracial relationship so publicly, much less have a child while in one. It was unheard of, and to some disgraceful. Dating outside of your race was just not socially acceptable, and to most it went against everything they were taught in Sunday school.

Though comments and stares were usually rude, the worst came from a little boy standing in the hallway watching the little girl watch her mother drive away from the daycare.

"I don't want that little nigger girl in my class!" shouted the boy. "My momma said it's a sin to be black with a white momma and I'm-a get a whoopin' if you're in my class."

This was the first time the little girl had ever met someone who outright hated the sight of her. It made her cry, not understanding why he was mad at her, what she had done. For the rest of the day, no one would play with her, talk to her, or even look at her. The teacher pretended the little girl didn't exist and wouldn't answer any of her questions. When her mother came to get her, she was sobbing.

"Don't make me go back, Momma," she cried. "Please, please, please! I'll be good, I promise! They were mean to me, Momma! Why were they mean? Did I do something wrong?"

The mother's biggest fears had come to life. They wouldn't accept her baby girl. It broke her heart to watch her baby cry over something she couldn't change no matter how hard she tried. It broke her heart even more to know she would have to take her back the next day and the following days after that.

As days grew into years and the girl grew older, the hateful comments didn't stop. They were just spoken in hushed tones and veiled behind kind words. People would say how lovely she was, but then talk about how they couldn't imagine being involved in a relationship with a mixed girl. Even friends would say there was nothing wrong with her, but they wouldn't dare bring home a "black" boy or girl home to meet Mom.

She couldn't find anything desirable or beautiful about herself, which her mom claimed she was every day. She wished her skin wasn't as rich of a tan as it was, her hair not as dark and curly. She longed to look like the other girls she saw in the hallway. Those girls were loved by everyone. They had boyfriends who would do anything for them. They could do anything with their hair and makeup. They, in her eyes, were perfect and all she strived to be but could never fully achieve. The young girl grew to hate herself more each day, the racist comments and hateful looks taking a toll on her self-esteem. She stopped believing what her mother said, spent less time in front of the mirror. Stopped trying to look nice, because what was the point? She would never look like the girls at her school. The ones loved by everyone.

Life and Afterlife

Alexis Etheredge

Throughout my life I have been asked to read many novels, whether they were of my choice or not. However, no book has inspired me throughout my life quite like *The Lovely Bones.*

Though it is fiction, *The Lovely Bones* has altered not only the way I look at life, but also the afterlife. By reading the accounts from the point of view of Susie, the deceased narrator, I learned how the grieving process affects many people, not just immediate family. Through her eyes I was able to watch how her death affected everyone she ever had contact with, how her father and sister never stopped searching for her, and how the boy she loved found it hard to move on without her. I learned that everything we do in life affects more than just the people involved. That life can end at any moment, through any means, so making the most of what I had left to live was more important than the latest trend.

This novel also challenged the way I saw heaven. Most people picture heaven as this pure oasis, where hate and prejudice don't exist. Everything is ivory and gold, with grand gates and streams of sunlight. However, after reading this novel, I believe that heaven is what you want it to be. It's not some general, massive, grand area of golden structures and white robes. To me heaven is a beach, with pure white sand and glasslike water. There are no harps or white-winged angels. It's an unembellished paradise, much like the narrator's heaven, which was only a field and large tree. Heaven doesn't have to be everyone's utopia. It has to be your paradise, your final resting place.

Even though *The Lovely Bones* is a thriller, a work of fiction, the message still made an impact on my life. Be careful of those you trust, because evil intentions can hide behind the most innocent of faces, but also push beyond the common beliefs of those around you. Don't view life as something filled with regrets and mistakes. Make the most of the time you are given, be memorable and worth missing. Create your own refuge, because it's your life and your oasis.

All of Them

Nicolas Fernandez

It was just a sad thing to watch. I had to go to her aid, even if I had told her I was busy. There's something about those flashing lights they leave on that upsets my stomach. Even the way they get out of their car is, I don't know, pretentious? She said, they said. She said, they said. *It's cold, the neighbors are watching, I have nothing to do with this. I want to go back home. Oh, she's crying now. Great. Now I have to stay.*

"Does she not know how to handle him at all? We're not here to be baby-sitters. We police adults," one of them told me.

Uh, I don't think she called by choice. And why are their police lights on again? Oh . . . of course.

"Are you his brother?" another one asked.

"No," I replied. Politely.

"She needs to be dealing with DJJ. We're wasting our resources here."

Umm, how exactly does a child running away equate to DJJ?

"Do you live *here*?" the same one continued.

"No. I'm just translating," I repeated. One of them sighed and looked around. My mother walked over. I was taking too long.

They asked for the woman's driver's license. "She doesn't drive," I told them.

"Whose car is this out front?" the other demanded.

How is this relevant?

"Her husband's," I lied. "He's not here right now."

They asked for other identification. The woman turned to me as she gave them the best she could. *Oh, there's the flashlight. It's not complete without their flashlight.* The officer returned her documents with an unappeased look on his face.

"Your ID?" he turned to me.

Uh, why? This was getting uncomfortable. I wanted a blanket. My mother scanned his face, then mine, trying to decipher the situation. She tugged at my shirt discreetly. I looked at the woman, then at their unfamiliar faces. Their offbeat voices, their intruding police radio sounds, their blinding car lights. *Why does this have a hospital connotation?* I felt that way even without a language barrier. I had to stay.

"It's at home. May I go get it?"

"Quick."

I heard a knock between their cruisers on my way. It was an officer at his window. He rolled it down. I had forgotten he was there.

"Hey, thanks for translating for her. That's really nice of you," he told me with a smile. It was a distracting, attractive smile. The warmth from his car replaced the cold of the night.

"Umm . . . thanks."

"Tell her thank you for calling us. We'll try our best to find her son."

"Will do."

I had to continue walking. It would have been inappropriate to laugh. Imagining my friend An's expected scolding for having thought about flirting had amused me.

"Guys suck. All of them," a disillusioned An would tell me.

"That's just your breakup speaking, An."

"It's my experience speaking."

"Don't let a bad apple spoil the bunch."

"This isn't just one."

"Oh, come on, the bad guys get all the hype."

"I can assure you the way I was treated did not get any hype. There may be some decent guys out there, but that doesn't mean I'm taking any chances."

"Aren't you being a little dramatic?"

"Prejudice doesn't arise spontaneously."

"What's funny is that you're telling all this to a guy."

Revelation on *Mango Street*

Nicolas Fernandez

"It's embarrassing," I remember thinking as a child when attending an event with my family. Not because of the usual child embarrassment but because of race. Translating from English to Spanish, feeling out of place and foreign, something I just didn't want to deal with, because, well, what is there to like about being Mexican?

Embarrassment, shame, and dislike of my background intensified as I aged. I was ashamed of Mexicans' sexist, homophobic, racist, and ignorant beliefs. I wanted to distance myself from being grouped with the "Mexicans."

Sandra Cisneros's *The House on Mango Street* ironically shined light on my own bigotry, prejudice, and negativity toward my background. It showed me the life and human spirit of what I labeled the bigoted, ignorant Mexican people. It called me to action and allowed me to take pride in my background and understand the humanity of everyone.

Not everyone is hateful, even if it appears that way. Yes, I often felt ostracized by my own family and people, but I read Cisneros's work and felt understood. She too felt trapped by the beliefs of her culture. I had someone of my own ethnicity to connect with at last. The author herself was someone who was the opposite of what I had usually associated with Mexicans. Her characters in *Mango Street* were also. Most of them weren't hateful or ignorant, just trapped. A life of having to quit school and work nonstop in grueling jobs is what many Mexicans are shoved into, and that background can limit their worldview. My point is that there are often reasons for why people act the way they do. One mustn't immediately jump to conclusions. Cisneros acknowledged that Mexicans have a "macho" culture that fosters sexism, but she didn't turn her disappointment into prejudice; she worked against it. Her character Esperanza defied this sexist culture. Cisneros's character showed me one can still be a part of one's ethnicity even when challenging the status quo.

Mango Street also changed my own subconscious belief that Mexicans are inferior. When calling home from school, I would hide in the corner and speak as quietly as possible because I was embarrassed to be heard speaking Spanish. After all, didn't that mean I had an "ignorant" mom who doesn't speak English? Cisneros's book showed me the hardships Mexicans go through. Undocumented immigrants disregarded and demonized regardless of their background, hopes and dreams rarely achieved due to monetary and/or educational barriers, living, as Esperanza put it, just looking out the window. Those things angered me. I saw her characters' life and optimism. They were full of pure life and pure, genuine attempts to be good but then saw their unfortunate destinies. I knew there was nothing inferior in their human spirit, and there certainly wasn't any way to justify their unfortunate destinies.

I was in awe of Sandra Cisneros's writing. She had the confidence to tell the stories of these Mexican Americans exactly as if they deserved nothing less than the conventional "American" story. Touched by her defense of her culture, I felt I had a duty to stand up for my people and for myself. It called me to action to call out hatred and prejudice and not to settle for less.

Living in a state dominated by a political party with a hateful ideology, with a state government that bars me from attending college here simply because I was brought to this country as a child through no fault of my own, definitely made me feel unvalued and disregarded. The Republican men get together to legislate in the General Assembly and pretend they're not full of prejudice. Cisneros allowed me to look past that and value myself, and also to not be afraid to confront that true bigotry. Cisneros showed me the power of literature and how much one can learn and change by picking up a book.

The Importance of Social Events

Maxwell T. Hall

I live in Anderson, South Carolina. Although it is a major city in South Carolina, it doesn't really feel like there are that many places for people to really meet. Sure, there are some wonderful events from time to time, such as the annual Starburst Storytelling Festival at my local library. But outside of annual or seasonal events, there doesn't really seem to be that many places where people can socialize. The main part of socialization is the gathering and interacting of people, and that is a very uncommon thing in this age of smartphones and devices. I think one good way to make South Carolina better is to have more facilities devoted to socializing.

As I was growing up, my parents took me out of the house to various places. They took me to the library, the theater, the park, and the arcade. My siblings would repeat my experiences, and we all ended up better for it. Through this socializing process, we had many experiences we never normally would have had, and we learned how to actually interact with other people. And that is what people never seem to do today: interact with other people. People spend so much time on the Internet, on their phones. They rarely go out and meet other people or try new things, which is why South Carolina should devote more effort to encouraging socialization.

Kid Venture, the park where my parents took me as a child, was one of my favorite places to visit. As the years went by and I grew older, I never lost my fondness for the park or the memories I made there. Sadly, it wasn't maintained as it should have been, and my family slowly stopped going there. I noticed many other people did the same thing, and the number of visitors seemed to decrease over the years. Later, my parents took me and my siblings to the Sheppard Swim Center. We were given swimming lessons, which taught us valuable lessons for the future. But that wasn't all it did. We were able to talk with the people who taught us, as well as the other students attending the swimming classes. It taught us how to speak with others and see that they were people who were just like us. It was an experience we wouldn't forget. And then the Sheppard Swim Center just closed one day and was promptly bulldozed.

Another place my family spent time was the arcade at the Anderson Mall. Now when we went to the mall, there were plenty of stores to visit. Only a few, such as the bookstore or the bath and beauty store, were stores we actually liked to visit. But the arcade was a true diamond in the rough. My parents would lead me there, and they'd show me all of these cool games lined up from wall to wall. There were ticket machines, and Skee-Ball machines, and arcade games of every genre and type. And there was even a place to exchange the ticket prizes for toys. My parents had told me about their own wonderful experiences in various arcades, and I got to see firsthand why they liked it so much. And the place was packed full of people who were just as happy as I. Except for the occasional spoiled child who was crying about something or other, there wasn't a frown to be had. But, like with most other things, the arcade just closed. One day it was there, the next it was gone.

And that is a big problem with South Carolina. All of these wonderful places that I visited were filled with people who were happy to meet and greet each other, and all of these places just seem to vanish for no reason. I don't know why. And the events where people actually can gather are either seasonal, like Halloween trick or treats, or happen so infrequently that most people wouldn't even know about them. These events could be absolutely wonderful for people. Look at the photographs of gatherings in the newspaper. It could be at a fairground, at an activity center, or even at the mall. You'll see people having fun, getting to know each other, and learning together. It creates bonds between people.

We need more places in South Carolina where people can socialize. We need more places in South Carolina where events can be held. We need to make it so that anyone, from children to adults and everyone in between, can share each other's memories, and in the process, create memories of their own. It would do wonders in making the state of South Carolina a better place.

Books—the Spark That Lights Imagination

Maxwell T. Hall

If there is one thing I love to do more than any other in this world, it is to read. Reading has helped me in countless ways. It has taught me, it has relaxed me, and it has intrigued me. But above all else, reading has inspired me to do something with my life. All of these writers in the world, from Steinbeck and Chaucer to Stephen King and Isaac Asimov, had a passion for their work. They showed me the wonders and creativity that existed in the worlds they created. And that helped mold me into the person I am today. One book that helped me more than any other in this regard is *Harry Potter and the Sorcerer's Stone*.

Now that book may not be an epic, thousand-page novel. It may not be the deepest or most emotional. But it is, without a doubt, an imaginative and enchanting story. It's full of wonder, the type of story to make the reader see the more imaginative side of things. I picked it up almost a decade ago, back when I was learning about the many things the world had to offer. And I was astounded.

Harry Potter and the Sorcerer's Stone is written in such a way that it seems so realistic, but you know it can't be. With all of the wizards, broomsticks, and potions, there's no way something like that could be real, right? You wouldn't know just by reading it, that's for sure. I learned from this book that you should never strive for pure realism all the time. You should take the time to think, to come up with bunches of exciting and imaginative things. That book showed me how to be open-minded.

Harry Potter and the Sorcerer's Stone definitely opened up a new world for me. Ever since I've read that book, I've thought a bit more "outside the box" with anything I've done. Even before reading it, I was a big fan of creating things. I love to draw, write, and design. I've been playing around with LEGO sets since I was three. I liked to scribble on the walls, because I thought it was amazing art. That Harry Potter book showed me that apart from doodling on the walls, I was right to have that creative streak. And it really got me thinking about something.

If J. K. Rowling could come up with such amazing places and characters, then what could I do? How could I actually express myself and my ideas? I took to drawing and writing, making my own comic books and graphic novels. I honed my craft and did the best job I could. Was the stuff I created actually good? Probably not; I don't really know. But I improved. I wanted to do better. And I practiced, day after day. I've made a point to get more creative with my school assignments and essays. Books like Harry Potter got me more interested in writing for contests, and a few years ago, I entered our local newspaper's Halloween writing contest. I won first place, and my prize was a Kindle. More important, the story was published in the *Anderson Independent-Mail,* which was pretty awesome. I wouldn't have even tried something like this high school writing contest if I hadn't been reading books like Harry Potter as a kid.

And now, ten years later, here I am. I'm ready for college and the future beyond that. I wouldn't have made it here without plenty of creativity and imagination. I have that book to thank for that. That's why I consider *Harry Potter and the Sorcerer's Stone* to be the most inspirational book I've ever read.

South Carolina's Other Prejudice

Andrew Herbst

In light of the challenging events that have occurred in South Carolina in 2015, the Palmetto State has responded with heart and positive reform. In July, following the devastating Charleston church shooting, Gov. Nikki Haley and the state legislature forced the removal of the Confederate flag from its inflammatory position in front of the statehouse. The change was necessary to combat the racism that continues to plague our state and country to this day. While the recent flooding led to seventeen deaths in our state, the response to the disaster demonstrated the great strength of our community and the protection we provide each other in times of need. The year has shown the spirit of South Carolina and led to improvements in the state, spanning areas from greater civil rights to stronger infrastructure.

Despite these improvements, a major demographic in our state is not being afforded the same advantages as another. As a state, we need to improve education, conditions, and opportunities for women and make them equal to those given to men. There is no excuse for the lack of equality between men and women, and for South Carolina to improve, we need to push for women's empowerment in several areas.

Education is an important component of empowerment. A part of education that has a direct connection to quality of life is sex education. As a student of the system, I can say the sex education curriculum in South Carolina suffers from a lack of connection with reality. To preserve innocence, the state has purged the curriculum of practical information that can help prevent disease and teen pregnancies. Instead of keeping kids innocent or pure longer, it just puts teenagers at a greater risk for issues associated with premarital sex. There are no benefits to this outdated curriculum. Our state legislature needs to allow schools to teach practical sex education to prevent teen pregnancy and disease. A limited education can lead to teen pregnancy, teen pregnancy leads to lower levels of education, and this malicious cycle continues. We need to update curriculum to keep our young women safe, unburdened, and on a path to higher education.

For the past ten years, South Carolina has remained one of the top ten states in the country for the number of women killed by men, as reported by the *Charleston Post and Courier* in 2014. This fact, along with other frightening domestic violence statistics, illustrates the desperate need for change in South Carolina. Women need to know that help is available if they feel threatened. The priority needs to be separating the victim from the attacker. First, more shelters need to be opened for victims. The lack of resources set aside for domestic abuse victims is appalling, and we need to allot more money to this cause in the state budget immediately. We also need to focus on higher prosecution rates for offenders. This will help teach kids, both boys and girls, that abuse is never acceptable. Finally children need to be taught at home and in school to respect themselves and others. If respect is understood, then abuse—and suffering from abuse—will decrease. It will help end the cycle of abuse in younger generations. Safety should not be conditional for anyone.

After securing a better education and safer living situation for women in South Carolina, we need to eliminate the gender wage gap. Our state is roughly on par with the national average, as reported by *Business News Daily*, with women earning seventy-eight cents for every dollar men earn. This is illogical and unfair, and our state legislature needs to pass laws that prohibit women being given disproportional pay. Empowerment in education is worth far less if women cannot be compensated fairly for their work. This is the easiest issue to solve and needs to be acted upon immediately to generate more interest in women in the workforce. The ability to generate income denotes an empowered person; that ability should not be restricted based on gender. Our legislature needs to take action now to stop unequal wages.

Many of the solutions proposed can be solved by strong legislative reform, and while this is necessary, improvements for women's empowerment start with respect at an individual level. Respect begets more respect. Respect, education, and equal opportunities will make South Carolina a better state for women and as a whole.

Ever-Changing Perspective

Andrew Herbst

Whether positive or negative, J. D. Salinger's novel *The Catcher in the Rye* always elicits a visceral response from readers. It has since it was first published in the 1950s, at a time when those in power requested that it be banned, and continues to do so in those who read it for the first time today. It is rare for a reader of this novel to be lukewarm about this stirring piece. The difference in my response was that my interpretation has changed drastically in the three times I've had the pleasure of reading it.

The differentiating factor of successful authors is the uncanny ability to draw out an intense feeling about their subjects. It does not matter the topic; a good author can make a reader get emotional about a cup of spilled milk. The reason I've read *The Catcher in the Rye* three times—when I never reread books or even rewatch movies—is Salinger has provoked such an adamant and passionate response from me each time. These multiple readings have increased my love for Salinger's work, yet have also demonstrated my emotional maturation and broader view of the world.

I first read *Catcher* in the seventh grade. Due to some unwarranted cynicism, I wholeheartedly identified with Holden Caulfield as a character. His frustration with those around him seemed equal to my own, and his ability to find the "phony" in people was a powerful trait. Holden Caulfield was my literary doppelgänger, and I loved Salinger's book, not for its redeeming qualities, but for Holden's lack of patience for what he perceives as ignorant or worthless. I had appreciated Salinger for the wrong reasons.

Upon a second read, I expected to love *Catcher* even more. However, I found that I was disgusted by Holden's lack of compassion and by his extreme impatience with everything he encountered. Holden does not see anything redeeming in anyone; he sees the worst and strives to bury his sorrow by criticizing others and hiding from the world. I found that I was disappointed in my twelve-year-old self as a reader for glancing over Holden's obvious psychological issues and his inability to find the positive in any aspect of his life. I threw down the Salinger with vigor and found it easy to dispel my previously positive regards about his most famous work.

As an assignment for school as a sophomore, I once again endeavored to read *The Catcher in the Rye*. Disheartened by my last reading, I thought I would find issue with the novel once more. Yet again, Salinger took me by surprise. Holden is neither a character to be championed nor a monster to be despised. He is at fault in many cases, but what drives these mistakes—failing out of prep schools, asking for money from his little sister's Christmas stash— is his inability to cope in society after his brother died so young. Combine his lack of coping ability with his despondent mother—a woman who had to bury her son—and he is obviously incapable of adjusting to his life without collateral damage. I castigated my younger selves for not recognizing the obvious signs of trauma Holden exhibits throughout Salinger's work. My earlier readings had been base and myopic and did not fully grasp the genius of the piece. Salinger's skill of evoking a response from his audience is predicated on his impressive ability to discuss emotion through the perspective of an imploding sixteen-year-old.

After analyzing *The Catcher in the Rye* for a third time, I recognized in myself a development that superseded my improvement in literary analysis. I realized I had achieved growth as a person. Having come to understand the root of Holden's erratic behavior, I grasped that I had improved in my capacity to be a compassionate, empathetic, and more patient person. My previous interpretations of the book illustrated my ignorance on a social level. I had been unable to understand others' behavior, and I had been unwilling to look for a cause behind their actions. Salinger helped me understand my ability to comprehend others. His work served as a gauge for my emotional growth.

Cursive Recurrence

Megan Jensen

Cursive writing. The beautiful, looped lines of a fading art form. Cursive is a classic style of writing that has been around for thousands of years, has numerous benefits, and should be brought back to South Carolina elementary school classrooms.

Cursive—also known as longhand, script, joint writing, looped writing, or running writing—dates to colonial days, when there was nothing to write with but quill and ink. The connected letters of cursive made writing much easier, allowing whole words to be written without lifting a hand from the page. Taught in schools since the start of formal education in America, the longhand style was dismissed as optional just several years ago. "Since 2010, 45 states . . . have adopted the Common Core standards, which do not require cursive instruction but leave it up to the individual states and districts to decide whether they want to teach it" (Shapiro). In schools' trying to follow nationwide-issued standards, this beautiful writing style may become obsolete. Why get rid of something that has been working for so long?

Neglecting such a beautiful skill could be dangerous, especially considering cursive has proven beneficial in more ways than one. The writing style aids in several different aspects of cognitive development. "When a child learns to read and write in cursive through consistent practice and repetition, he or she must effectively integrate fine motor skills with visual and tactile processing abilities" (Brain Benefits). Incorporating the visual of the letters, palpable practice of writing the ABCs, and the connection of letters into words and sentences is a kind of therapy for children, especially those with dyslexia. Learning longhand allows for a steady, persistent ritual that can better the lives of children with this disorder. Dyslexia stems from a breach in communication between the auditory and language centers of the brain, and the tactile writing method helps children better retain what they learn. Higher grades and test scores also have been linked to the longhand practice, as concluded by Laura Dinehart, assistant professor of early childhood education at Florida International University. Neater handwriting leads to more developed reading and math skills, which present themselves in SAT scores. According to a 2006 College Board Report, of all the SATs taken in the country, 15 percent of the essay portions are written in cursive. Those included in the 15 percent received slightly higher scores than their printed counterparts.

I grew up in Minnesota and learned cursive writing in the third grade. To this day I write in cursive and am proud of my swooping letters and perfected signature. Yet I notice many of my classmates are uneducated in the art of cursive writing and often fall behind in notetaking compared to me. I credit my quickness to the fact that I write in cursive rather than print. In this increasingly mechanized society, the longhand form of writing is becoming a lost art. Many schools are so busy teaching kids about technology that they dismiss the importance of the basics.

Though many schools are still teaching cursive, the students are not getting the amount of practice time needed (Zezima). Most schools where cursive instruction is still included teach the longhand form for limited amounts of time. The current ineffectiveness may also be credited to the fact that cursive is not often taught after third grade. The lack of reinforcement allows for the skill to slowly ooze out of memory until it reverts back to a foreign language and remains that way.

The ancestry of the writing style often is viewed negatively as old and outdated, but to me, the heritage shows how treasured and respected longhand is. A signature is an embellishment of self. An accessory to shape someone into an individual and make each and every person one of a kind. Bringing cursive back into elementary classrooms is a vital step in allowing children to become unique individuals with a strong sense of self.

Works Cited

Cohen, Jennie. "A Brief History of Penmanship on National Handwriting Day." History.com. A&E Television Networks. 23 Jan. 2012. Accessed 31 Oct. 2015.

Hruby, Kate. "Reading (Writing) between the Lines." *Greenwood (S.C.) Index-Journal.* 2 Dec. 2012. Accessed 30 Oct. 2015.

Klemm, William R. "Biological and Psychology Benefits of Learning Cursive." *Psychology Today.* 5 Aug. 2013. Accessed 31 Oct. 2015.

Peper, Warren. "Cursive Handwriting Declining but Still Has Value." *Charleston (S.C.) Post and Courier.* 3 Mar. 2015. Accessed 30 Oct. 2015.

Shapiro, T. Rees. "Cursive Handwriting Is Disappearing from Public Schools." *Washington Post.* 4 Apr. 2013. Accessed 30 Oct. 2015.

"Write Cursive for Brain Development." Brain Balance Achievement Centers. 17 Sept. 2014. Accessed 31 Oct. 2015.

WYFF4. "Bill to Require SC Students Learn Cursive Advances." 19 Mar. 2014. Accessed 30 Oct. 2015.

Zezima, Katie. "The Case for Cursive." *New York Times.* 27 Apr. 2011. Accessed 31 Oct. 2015.

Extremely Insightful and Incredibly Life-Changing

Megan Jensen

I don't believe novels have to call you to physical action to incite change. Change can be as simple as looking at the world through a new set of eyes. Reading a book allows you to see what the author sees and feel what the author feels. As an avid reader and lover of literature, trying to pin down one single book that has prompted me to evaluate my thinking or actions is a difficult task. Everything I've ever read has inspired some sort of change in my life or way of thinking. The most recent of all the change-inciting works of literature I've read is *Extremely Loud and Incredibly Close* by Jonathan Safran Foer.

Foer writes from an incredibly unique perspective but still is able to relate to an array of readers. He writes through the point of view of an emotionally burdened child who has just tragically lost his father in the terrorist attacks of 9/11. *Extremely Loud and Incredibly Close* makes you wonder what's going on in the heads of others. After reading this book, I often find myself looking at strangers in passing, wondering what they've gone through in their lives and how those events have affected their life choices and direction.

I've always been an emotionally sensitive person, caring deeply about the feelings of friends and family around me, but *Extremely Loud and Incredibly Close* opened my mind and eyes to people not in my immediate circle. It's not that I was unaware of the feelings experienced by people I don't know; I just didn't think anything of them. My demeanor and the way I think about and act toward others has changed dramatically since reading this book. The cliché phrase "Don't judge a book by its cover" is proven by *Extremely Loud and Incredibly Close* in a metaphorical sense as well as a physical one. You don't expect a book with a red hand on the front to be about a 9/11 loss, just as you don't expect a person who looks calm and collected on the outside to be falling apart on the inside.

I haven't gone out with great plans to become a missionary or therapist, but I have noticed a difference in my day-to-day thoughts and treatment of others. How can change happen on a large scale if it doesn't start smaller? Small acts of change are what keep the big acts going. A change in perspective is constant. It is gradual but becomes permanent and lasting. A monumental dose of random passion is great for the moment, but it's fleeting. Far too often a large act of change burns out and fizzles back down to day-to-day dullness.

Without thought, creativity and revolutionary change would not prevail. Static would overpower, and innovation would cease to exist. Thinking is absolutely necessary for any form of advancement to occur and is the reason we can change, thrive, and create.

Extremely Loud and Incredibly Close has changed my worldview and opened me up to feelings and emotions I never imagined possible. The way I think has been transformed by the characters and themes within. This novel has found a home in my mind, and I have thought about it constantly since the day I turned the last page.

The Girl with the Butterfly Clips

Abby Johanson

She always wore tiny butterfly clips in her hair, which was fitting as I rarely heard her speak. Besides being in three classes together and passing her along the halls, in the lunch room, even outside in the parking lot, she never made a sound.

She floated when she walked, trying to desperately slip around people without brushing up against them, her footsteps silent, her gait awkward. I could tell it was her greatest desire to not be seen, to blend into the background so no one would notice her; a trampled little flower trying to regrow her stem.

I noticed, though.

And to the butterfly girl's desperation, so did everyone else.

She arrived in the middle of the semester, wrapped in a thick pink sweater. Even as the teacher introduced her, I could hear the snickers from the back of the room radiating out to the front like scalding solar radiation.

Her cheeks flamed red, making them snicker even more. She stood awkwardly, pigeon-toed, a bright red, freckled tomato as the teacher patted her shoulder, addressing the rest of the class in long monotone sentences.

I felt sorry for her.

The first time I heard her speak was during the pandemonium of a lunch period, three weeks after she arrived. She was walking through the forest of tables, a pile of books held tight to her chest. She was quietly making her way toward the doors when a leg slipped out from one of the tables, tripping her at the last second, sending her crashing to the floor, a loud crescendo of books and papers.

The room went from a deafening rumble to an eerie silence. She didn't look up. She knew the outstretched leg was a predatory attack from a pack of teenage girls. She knew exactly where the leg had come from.

"Better look where you're going."

"Yeah, you'd better clean up this mess."

"*Trash.*"

She was scrambling to grab all the papers that had flooded the floor, picking up the dirt, grime, and overall filth associated with a thousand seventeen-year-olds. She grew smaller and smaller, cocooning more with each snide comment.

Without a thought, I bent down and picked up a handful of the papers. When my eyes met hers, she immediately dropped her gaze to the floor as she shrank smaller and smaller, the voices smothering her with suffocating conceit.

I gave her a sad, half-hearted smile before extending the now-crumbled stack of papers toward her.

"Thank you."

The words that slipped out were quieter than the rustling of a butterfly's wings, and then she was gone, disappearing into the crowds like a shadow in the cover of darkness. I could feel the others' eyes on me, but I turned back to my table, my friends.

She was like a kicked puppy, injured, afraid, and as soon as she could she scampered out of striking range.

I wouldn't really call it bullying; it was only one girl. The teachers had more important things to worry about: test scores coming back, unfortunate, time-consuming changes in Common Core, the newest selection of mystery meat in the cafeteria.

So they didn't help her.

Her presentation was on seashells.

Our speech and debate teacher insisted on the values of positive feedback, clap for your classmates, applaud for your peers, leave no student behind. So after every presentation we clapped, even if it was a slow clap, a bored, pity clap.

She spoke softly, eyes glued to the back wall of the classroom as she quietly wove a tale of her family's home on the water, which they lost to the recession, and of their beach vacations. When she finished, there was a pause. And the silence that followed was foggy and filled with anticipation. I turned to see one of the student council members move first, standing up silently and turning around to face the back wall.

The message was clear.

And one by one, the rest of the students in the class followed her.

I felt my body grow heavy like lead in my desk. Her eyes met mine from across the room. The blue in them shined brighter with the withheld tears. The pleading in them was so heavy and thick it was tangible in the air; thick like a smoke snake squeezing, suffocating my insides.

I stood up and turned around.

It Started on Page 4

Abby Johanson

It began on page 4—a sort of flutter in the sides of my stomach, a tingling in my fingertips that I couldn't ignore.

By chapter 4 the tingling had spread up my arms, roving mercilessly like a thousand fire ants crawling toward my heart.

It wasn't until the middle of the novel (perhaps page 394) that I realized I *liked* the feeling. The pages were thick, heavy with the tears fallen from previous readers, the adrenaline spilled from sweaty brows over the author's words. I'm pretty sure there was blood stuck to the final chapters—sticky, wet, and oddly exuberating.

"You must read this book!" my friend had begged me one afternoon. She had always been a good friend, so I listened; I just never expected the hardback book to break my heart.

J. K. Rowling's story—you know the one—wove an inexplicably wonderful, captivating world from which I truly never left.

Her ability to create a battle so realistically relevant and touching has given me the greatest example of literary expectation to hold my craft up to. Like a weaver she masterfully bound and tied so many intimate, human characters' stories into a single well-executed plot, leaving no stray threads. She shows every writer the meaning of the phrase "plot twist" while shattering everything you thought you knew about a character—and building a better, more beautifully broken mosaic.

The Harry Potter books—as analyzed by my eleven-year-old self—made me want to be a writer, to be able to so carefully craft a story that could make readers weep, no matter their age or race or socioeconomic class. Make them identify with their humanity. And prove no matter the circumstances—jealous, entitled bullies, deaths of loved ones, or the entire fate of the Wizarding World on your shoulders—that love always conquers evil.

Good books—truly good books—are not one-theme, one-character to every reader. Harry Potter advocates the underdog, the underloved, the overlooked, and the nobodies. True beauty isn't reflected in societal, sparkly vampires or overly sexualized scandal but in hand-me-down glasses repaired with friendship and sacrificial chess moves.

It taught me that in the end, and in the future, the cast-outs like Harry, the know-it-alls like Hermione, and the looked-overs like Ron always end up on top.

On page 4, I knew something special began on Number Four Prince Drive. (I found my home.)

Unspoken Cries

Katherine Kristinik

One class on one day in one middle school is beginning, and the paths of several students converge in one classroom.

Daniel is full of anxiety as the school bus pulls up to school. He knows his class will be reading a book out loud today, but he struggles to read. *How did I make it this far?* he thinks. *I want to ask for help, but I don't know how. In a class of thirty kids, what difference does it make that I can't read?* It's difficult enough to try to read in English, but adding dyslexia to the mix makes it impossible. Daniel's favorite class is Spanish. He knows exactly what is going on because he comes from a Spanish-speaking family. He enjoys helping other students in class and talking with the teacher. If only someone would tell Daniel how great a teacher he would be.

Qui Qui is full of worry as she walks to school. Her grades are low, and her parents and teachers continually chide her to do better. But she is not passionate about school; she is passionate about art. She respects the artist Mark Rothko for his ability to create a painting that makes her feel a range of emotions. She aspires to do that, but her art class is elementary and dull, and she continually looks for a challenge. Her school has a low budget, and the money is distributed to the academic classes first, the ones she is not succeeding in. She has felt her self-expression get pent up inside, and she isn't sure how much longer she can take it. If only someone had given Qui Qui the time to be an artist.

Marcus is full of hopelessness as the bus arrives at school. He comes from a broken family, and he knows he is stuck in the cycle, so why bother with school? He only goes for the lunch, which he saves to bring home to his mother and sister. Actually he doesn't mind math class. In math there is always a formula, and there is always an answer. Everything makes sense. But he lacks a father figure, and while he respects his mother for working all the time, it is difficult for him to find motivation to try in school, so even though he doesn't detest math, his grade is low from missing homework and not studying. If only someone had stepped in as a mentor and told Marcus, *you can break the cycle; you can do it.*

Kathleen is full of self-doubt as the bus pulls up. She wonders why she tries in school, because there are so many people who are better than she is. They are going to be the successful ones, she thinks. She often expresses her feelings about this through writing, which is quite good. This is not reflected in her English class, because they analyze books and poetry. *Why can't we write just to write?* she thinks. There is a standardized test coming up soon, and she is worried because she doesn't test very well. In her diary that day, she wonders how anything can be standardized, because people are all different, with different talents, most immeasurable by a test. *Does testing badly on the writing section mean I'm a bad writer?* If only someone had told Kathleen she was a good writer, maybe she wouldn't have doubted herself as much.

The bell rings, and the class meets for the day. Each child comes with his or her individual struggles and strengths, but their struggles are highlighted, and their strengths asphyxiate under a blanket of "do better." The children work so hard to fix their weaknesses that they leave their strengths to rust. If they home in on their strengths, they would gain motivation.

Their school could also provide help for when the children go home. Because the children spend more time at home than school, providing some outreach to families or mentoring and tutoring for children in all schools would be an amazing resource that could change a child's perspective. Middle school is a time of finding yourself, and a child is still at the age where he or she can be molded and change shape with the smallest act of kindness or smallest act of cold-heartedness. School is so influential, and this one class represents the future, so schools should be of the highest quality possible to motivate students to take action for their futures.

With help from the schools, Daniel can grow in confidence, Qui Qui can express herself, Marcus can gain courage to keep trying, and Kathleen can find hope to keep writing instead of quitting. These could be very real students in a very real school, and their futures depend on the very real changes that need to be made by lawmakers.

How I Define Living

Katherine Kristinik

Am I living or surviving? Although my English class was applying this question to the novel *Catch-22* by Joseph Heller, I applied it to my life. In the novel, the difference between the two is established by a soldier in a full body cast who is observed by the character Yossarian. Yossarian sees that the soldier is completely isolated from the world around him because he cannot speak or move. My situation is not as dire as the soldier's, but I pondered this idea. Am I taking advantage of all the opportunities around me? I look to my right and hear my friends listing the various things they have to do in too short of a time. I may not be as involved as they are, I think to myself, but if that is living, it sure seems stressful. I look left at the student sitting next to me. Smart, athletic, has many friends. That seems like the balance I'm looking for. I wish I had that.

However, when I look inward and think of all the experiences I have had, I believe I am living instead of simply doing enough to survive. The first thing I think of is zip lining in Costa Rica with my classmates. I jump off the platform, and suddenly, I am aware of the fact that I am alone. I am so high in the air, and the wind is so loud; the trees are so green, and the lake is so big. I am reminded of when Yossarian watches his friends fly in from a mission from the beach. He remembers who he is, and his thoughts and feelings as a person are affirmed when his friends are around him. Differently from Yossarian, I am reminded of my existence when I am alone. When there isn't anyone to turn to and say, "Are you scared of jumping off the platform?" I'm in my own head, where anything can be true, and my thoughts are unsaid to everyone but myself.

Individualism is something that distinguishes Yossarian, and I find that inspiring. A uniform is important to the military, but Yossarian chooses not to wear it. Even though he is in the midst of World War II, he also is not afraid to ask about being sent home when he has completed the number of aerial missions he was asked to do. His choices demonstrate to me that when I am alone, zipping over treetops, I shouldn't be afraid of being left with myself. I have valid thoughts and feelings that are completely my own, and I don't need someone to validate them, but it's okay to commiserate or celebrate or share my thoughts because I can find a support group, like Yossarian's friends, who can help my confidence grow to make a change. The different quirks of Yossarian's friends make the novel so enjoyable, and I have acquired an extreme desire to meet quirky people. They make life much more interesting. This is one of the ways I hope to make my life one about living instead of surviving.

An aspect about our society that I think emphasizes surviving over living is the constant battle to be the best. In school it is the battle to get the best grades. In society it is the battle to be the richest and most attractive. In the case of Yossarian's squadron, it is the battle to complete the most aerial missions and attain the highest military rank. Yossarian is indifferent toward the ranks and sees them as another way that the military calls men to conform. The battle for an arbitrary rank or number in school emphasizes gaining something over someone. The idea of living is not being better than others but achieving an insight or becoming the best person you can be. To me, living is existing with other people, and surviving is existing in spite of other people. I look forward to living with people who will add spice to my life and help me grow as a person, so I can achieve contentment with myself.

The Dreamer

Jared Mack

It's a cold day in Andrews, South Carolina, and in this small town lives a boy. He is no ordinary boy. He wants to do big things, but he's afraid of the world. He is insanely smart, but he limits his smarts to fit in with the popular classmates. The boy has talent, but he can't see the error of his ways. It will definitely take more than just some talking to get him to open his eyes and see the world. To the boy's surprise, this discovery will start with a simple paper ball.

Pop! The paper ball pops the math teacher with an unexpected sting. The teacher turns from his lesson to see fingers point at a nappy-haired black boy with a shameless grin on his face.

"Oooooh, Ben! You're about to get it!" says one of his classmates.

"Don't kill him, Mr. Millbrook!" shouts a girl from the far corner.

Mr. Millbrook has a looming presence. He walks up to Ben and bends over to whisper in his ear. "See me after class," he whispers. Mr. Millbrook straightens up and walks back to the board. He could hear the kids laughing and whispering among themselves. "Now, can anyone solve for v?"

After class, while all the kids scramble out the small door, Ben sits at his desk, anxious. Mr. Millbrook sits at his desk.

"Ben, come here," he says.

Ben stiffly gets up and takes a seat at the teacher's desk. Mr. Millbrook smiles at the boy to reassure him. All the smile does is make the boy more anxious.

"Do you know why I asked you to stay after class?"

Ben slowly nods. "I attacked you with a paper ball," he says.

"Correct, Mr. Walker!" Mr. Millbrook smiles. He pulls out a pink piece of paper and a test paper with a 100 score on it. "Now answer me on this. What is this?"

Ben looks at both papers. "It is a discipline slip and our last test," he answers.

"So what do you think I'm trying to say, Mr. Walker?"

Ben continues to analyze the two papers. He shrugs his shoulders.

Mr. Millbrook comically slaps his head. "I'm trying to say you're limiting yourself, Mr. Walker. This pink slip shows the limit barrier you've placed on yourself."

Ben looks at the teacher with disgust. "Who are you to tell me who I am, Mr. Millbrook?"

"No, Mr. Wal—" Mr. Millbrook tries to intervene but Ben cuts him off. "Don't you see my grade? I clearly got things under control!"

Ben starts to walk out, but Mr. Millbrook catches his attention with one sentence. "You are more than this town."

Ben freezes. "You are more than the thugs you listen to. I see you in class. You want to answer every question I ask but you're afraid of the life," Mr. Millbrook preaches. "You are afraid that your friends will tease you and disown you. You are one of the smartest children I've seen pass through these doors, but you limit your potential so you can bang your guns and females."

Ben sits down in the chair. He turns to his teacher. His eyes are misty. "I want to be better, but I fear it sometimes," he says.

Mr. Millbrook nods. "I can help you out, Mr. Walker."

"What can you do, Mr. Millbrook?" Ben asks.

"Here's my offer," Mr. Millbrook says, sliding a pamphlet toward Ben.

Ben looks at the pamphlet. "Why should I care if I go anywhere anyways?" he says. "Our state's education sucks."

Mr. Millbrook shakes his head. "I think differently, Mr. Walker," he replies. "You see, education is like a bicycle. We are the handles, you guys are the pedals. Correct?"

Ben looks at the pamphlet and smiles. "So . . . MATHletes?"

Mr. Millbrook nods and smiles.

3 Months Later

Ben Walker stares at his math competition trophy and smiles. He moves in motion with the rocking bus, full of his seated MATHlete teammates and their coach, Mr. Millbrook. Ben walks up to the front where Mr. Millbrook sits and taps him on the shoulder.

"Yes, Mr. Walker?" Mr. Millbrook says, pulling out his earbuds.

"Thanks, Mr. Millbrook," Ben says.

"What for, Benjamin?"

Ben grins and responds. "For saving me."

Don't limit your potential.

Caged Birds

Jared Mack

Truthfully not a lot of books inspire me. But if I had a choice, it would have to be the Maya Angelou book *I Know Why the Caged Bird Sings*. Typically a book about a poor girl who doesn't have much and goes through a lot wouldn't interest a teenage boy like me. However, the book oozes a certain type of intellect and fire that I enjoy. It may not be an action novel or a comedy, but it's a tale of survival and discovery.

When I first read this book, I was forced by my mom to read it as a summer reading assignment. Of course I was angry and disgusted that I had to read such a girly-looking book. But this was before I read it. Once I got the hate out of my heart, I opened a book and allowed it to really inspire me. Despite our many differences, the main character and I had a lot in common. She was curious about the world, just like me. She was adventurous, also like me. Plus she had a lot of heart despite the odds and obstacles, just like me also.

This book inspired me because it featured the view of a black person in the South. Even with the more equality blacks are given today, there is still a constant force that stops blacks from where they want to be. In the book there is an everlasting struggle between blacks and whites. This really opened my eyes to the cruelty my ancestors faced. Today we don't face the same kinds of problems that blacks in the 1950s faced, but we still have enormous problems. A good example (and frequently used one) is the Black Lives Matter campaign. The police brutality that African Americans face has been going on forever, even through the time period of *I Know Why the Caged Bird Sings*. The book's excellent imagery and dialogue show many readers, of any race, how hard it was to be black.

In all honesty, I don't read as much as I should. But when I do read, I hope those books can stick onto my heart like this book does. *I Know Why the Caged Bird Sings* is a compelling story of survival, humor, and humility. It shows more than a little girl. It also shows her scars. The book also shows how and why Maya Angelou was one of the greatest African American authors of all time.

Fine Arts

Why Are They Important?

Milner Martin

Many people don't believe the fine arts do anything to help with test scores. The fine arts are very important when it comes to better test scores. They have been around for many years. Without the fine arts, how would we be communicating with each other to this day? Theater is a great example of how we use the fine arts to learn a little bit of everything. Even math and science are learned within this category. It teaches students other elements of education without them even realizing it. We learn how to support one another within the fine arts. They also help develop strong social skills.

There is a difference between art and fine art. Fine art pertains to beauty and communication, while art is simply the practice of artistic skills. It helps us express who we really are. It gives us a sense of escape from the real world around us. Without things like art, theater, music, and other things that give us simple joys in life, what would be the point of living?

Larry Shiner, a professor of visual arts at the University of Illinois, explains that fine arts date as far back as the eighteenth century. When I actually think about it, the fine arts are the reason why we can communicate. Painting has been around since the beginning of mankind. Cavemen used it as a form of communication. They would draw animals being hunted on the walls of their caves or the side of a mountain. As time passed, man became more and more intelligent. Eventually a language was created. We started to use hand motions to express what we wanted to say. Eventually we learned how to write as well. This eventually evolved into what we know as "theater."

We may not know it, but theater actually teaches us a little bit of every-thing. We can learn math, new vocabulary terms, writing techniques, and economics—almost anything! Reading various Shakespeare plays may inspire you to write in your own unique style. However, we do not realize we are learning these other things while we are trying to produce or read a play. If you are given the lead part in a play, you are expected to learn a lot of lines. Within these lines, there will almost always be a vocabulary term you may not know. As an actor, your job is to find out what that word means so that you can express its meaning in the right way.

In theater you aren't always just learning about literature. You learn a bit of math and science as well. If a director told you to stand 45 degrees toward another actor onstage, how would you do this? Simple! You would turn your body to face between the actor and the audience, because halfway between 0 and 90 is 45. Yes, this is actually used in theater. When working in theater, you might also become a technician. You could be in charge of lighting and sound. If you're a producer, you have to know how to manage the many people you need to produce your show. As you can see, everything sort of blends together.

In the fine arts, you also build a strong community and learn how to give and get support from others. You can't have a football team without a quarter-back. The same can be applied to fine arts. In theater, chorus, and other forms of fine art, you need a strong group of people you know you can depend on. You can't have a theatrical performance without the extras or the lead charac-ters. You can't have a choir without the tenors and sopranos. In the fine arts, you learn how important it is to follow up on something that you have com-mitted your time to. People depend on you. If you let those people down, you will learn that you may not be trusted to get the lead part again. You may not be able to get that solo you have always wanted in chorus.

One of the most important things the fine arts might do for us is develop social skills. It is always a good thing to be able to perform onstage in front of an entire audience. This can help us get over stage fright. We won't be afraid to make the next public announcement. We will no longer be afraid to show off our musical talents that we work so hard on.

The fine arts are crucial in both our education and social systems. Accord-ing to many educational websites, such as Parenting.com, the fine arts make us smarter, more independent, individuals. Without "art," earth would just be . . . "Eh" . . .

Works Cited

"Art and Communication." *Art & Perception.* http://artandperception.com/2006/11/art-and-communication.html.

Kalish, Nancy. "Why Art Makes Kids Smarter." *Parenting.* https://www.parenting.com/article/why-art-makes-kids-smarter.

Shiner, L. E. *The Invention of Art: A Cultural History.* Chicago: U of Chicago P, 2001.

Learning from a Tragedy

Milner Martin

There is a saying in theater: "There are no small parts, only small actors." William Shakespeare's *Romeo and Juliet* is a tragedy. While many people believe the tragedy is in Romeo's and Juliet's deaths, it actually goes a bit deeper. Two households have a strong dislike for one another. Romeo and Juliet happened to have fallen into those two separate households. However, they want no part in their family tradition. This play has inspired me to stand up for what is right, and hopefully it has for many others as well.

Romeo and Juliet have been raised to hate one another in much the same way we are taught by some religions that gay marriage is wrong. However, they do not follow this rule. Instead, Romeo and Juliet slowly start to realize the rules that have been set forth are wrong. There is something to be said about their passion to overcome something that seems nearly impossible to accomplish.

The real tragedy in this play is the reactions of various characters. They represent the society they live in, though it is clear the society they live in is wrong. Lady Capulet, Juliet's mother, becomes outraged when Juliet tells her she would rather marry Romeo than Paris. However, because Lord Capulet believed Paris was a wealthy nobleman, he had already arranged Juliet's marriage to Paris. Juliet knows this is not how things should be, so she rebels against her parents. She goes against everything she was taught.

How can one not be inspired by this play? To speak up for yourself. To take action, even when your entire family, friends, and the world itself is against you. One day, you'll realize one of two things: you have to take a stand for what is right, or regret not doing so years later. This play can be an inspiration for young people to stand up for what is right. If there is a pastor who is preaching something from the Bible that is taken out of context, then you should say something about it. If the principal of a high school plans on expelling someone for something you know they didn't do, then you should speak up for that person.

Looking back at one of the greatest plays of all time, *Romeo and Juliet,* we can easily be inspired to take action for something we know is wrong. Romeo and Juliet go against everything they have been taught to believe to be with the one they love. While it results in tragic deaths, they made a positive change in their society. Let *Romeo and Juliet* be a source of inspiration for all who are afraid to stand up and take action for what they know is right.

Recommended Strategies to Ignite Economic Growth

Isis McNeal

Our politicians are elected not to impose their will on the people, but to represent those who put them in office. Everything would be simple if we upheld that single principle. This is not an attack on the political system, merely an objection to tactics that do not induce change in our economy. It is my deep-seated belief that South Carolina has the potential to produce an economic miracle akin to the swift transformation of Dubai into one of the most sought-after destinations in the world. I am by no means implying that we strive to achieve such lofty goals, but we must take into consideration our economic well-being. Hence I have devised an economic development plan which, if implemented, will result in the improvement of the overall state economy. I knew that by submitting this essay, it was the only way to get my voice heard.

Encourage Entrepreneurship. Nothing drives economic growth like entrepreneurs and their startups. We can assist entrepreneurs in their early days by setting up business incubators. This can easily be created by a group of likeminded citizens or the local chamber of commerce. This doesn't require the construction of a new building, either. You can renovate abandoned downtown properties.

Attract other companies. By consistently networking with major corporations, we can convince them to set up headquarters in our region. This is how megalopolises are created. Also consider the countless jobs that will be created. Lure them here by informing them we are a right-to-work state.

Find a niche market. Georgia, for example, provides production incentives for film directors who shoot their movies within its borders. This has enabled the film and TV industry to thrive so much that TV productions have generated an economic impact of $6 billion in Georgia. Let's find that one factor that could have a huge impact on the number of jobs created.

Environmental Initiatives. I'm an environmentalist, so I think we should set our sights on becoming the greenest state in the South. I favor more curbside pickup recycling programs. On another note, our countryside offers the relaxation we take for granted. We can appeal to those who are trying to escape the fast-paced city life in need of a vacation.

Establish a youth council. Did you know that in Europe the United Nations hosts a youth council where young adults can express their concerns and share ideas about what can be done to improve their countries? Here a youth advisory council could inform their mayors of what their communities lack and how those needs can be met. Or they could simply attend a council meeting and present what's on their minds. Who better to turn to than the youth? This is not to discredit adults but to acknowledge that young people are the most valuable technology consumers, according to www.inc.com, and therefore play a significant role in the success or failure of an investment. Via social media, teens promote businesses whether they realize it or not.

As someone who grew up in the suburbs of Atlanta, I can tell you from firsthand experience that it's hard to make a difference when everything is going well. There is no difference to make. But here the story is different. We South Carolinians have the opportunity to make an opportunity. This is why I can't help but see my future here. I might've been molded with red Georgia clay, but South Carolina now has my heart, mind, and soul.

Some will say because of the recent flooding that these are just more goals that won't be achieved anytime soon. Let me assure those by reminding you of an historical event: Sherman's March to the Sea. This act literally left the city of Atlanta in a pile of dust. Yet Georgians weren't having it; they wanted their city back. What they ended up with is more than they could've ever dreamed. They quickly rebuilt their precious hub, and to this day, Atlanta is dubbed "the city too busy to hate." Remember it's not the circumstances, but how you respond to them. Here's a little poem I wrote to sum up why we can't give up on ourselves:

> South Carolina is the best place for me
> The Palmetto State is where I want to be.
> Even when I'm old, and my hair's all gray
> Thirty years from now you'll still hear me say,

I'm just not leaving
'Cause it makes sense to stay.
Probably not at this moment
Or this time and place
But have some patience
Rome wasn't built in one day.

The Ultimate Mentor Book

Isis McNeal

Books are akin to schoolteachers. Throughout our lives, we will have many teachers. However, there is always that one teacher who tells you your purpose in life. The Chicken Soup for the Soul series is similar to that motivational teacher. As the title suggests, it is written specifically for your soul. Did you catch that? This is not your typical self-help book that only informs you of what you subconsciously already know.

Each book is a collection of true stories that cause you to reconsider everything you thought you knew about life. As your eyes scan the pages, you are completely immersed in the story before you. You enter a state of mind that transcends reality, because the book will grasp your attention so much that without warning the left side of your brain has disappeared. You are now left with the often-abandoned right side of your brain, or what's popularly known as your imagination.

Neurologists claim that we're only using ten percent of our brain. How can we expect innovative change when the mind-set required to produce that change is frowned upon? That's why *Chicken Soup for the Soul* is the book that has brought out the best in me. In fact, it was instrumental to me submitting my first response to the South Carolina High School Writing Contest. Jack Canfield, the coauthor of these inspiring books, is also a well-known motivational speaker. He has no need to speak, though, for you can hear his voice in his writing. I first stumbled upon this book series during my freshman year of high school. The first book of this series I read was titled *Chicken Soup for the Teenage Soul*. As I read, I was confounded by the fact that the material was completely relatable to teens. It helped me overcome adolescent challenges, because I learned how to handle issues such as popularity, dating, grades, and rumors in a constructive manner—for example, exercising or joining clubs.

One particular story, "I Am Home," pertains to Julia, a teenage girl who was raised with seven siblings on a family-owned ranch. Though an ordinary teen would view raising livestock as a tiring chore, Julia considered it to be highly desirable. Tragically her dad suffered a severe heart attack that prohibited him from participating in any more strenuous activity. The family was forced to kiss their ranch life goodbye. Julia goes on to explain that although she adapted pretty well to her new urban environment, she realized that it couldn't compare to the tranquil countryside.

Eventually Julia returned to a rural setting in her adult life. While that story might not seem extraordinary, it proves the old adage to be true: there's no place like home.

It Is Time to Fix Our Roads and Bridges

Aimee McVey

At the time the Cumberland Road was constructed in the early 1800s, few Americans imagined a United States crisscrossed with highways and two-lane roads connecting every town and city. When the first Model T rolled off the assembly line in Detroit, the masses only dreamed of owning such luxury. By the time Dwight D. Eisenhower implemented the Interstate Highway System in 1956, the automobile had become ingrained in the American way of life. Now, sixty years later, our roads are crumbling, falling into a state of disrepair that increases every passing year without repairs. South Carolina is the sixth most dangerous state to drive in, according to Foxbusiness.com. Potholes mar long stretches of road, resulting in flat tires and broken axles, and bridges are barely deemed passable. There is no doubt that the cost to citizens, in more frequently needed repairs and traffic accidents, dramatically increases with poor road conditions. South Carolina must take action to provide safer roads and bridges for its drivers.

Just how much are South Carolina drivers affected? The Road Information Program (TRIP) tells us that deficient roads cost motorists more than $1,200 per year, a price including operating costs and time lost due to traffic jams. Moreover problems with vehicle control due to road conditions lead to more accidents. The South Carolina Department of Transportation states that one car accident occurs every 4.7 minutes, and the National Highway Traffic Safety Administration reports that South Carolina leads the nation in fatal wrecks per 100 million miles traveled. The need for improvement is obvious, yet the South Carolina House and Senate refuse to cooperate on the issue. It is time to compromise, and it is time to fix our roads and bridges.

One of South Carolina's primary sources of revenue is tourism. Not many people want to drive five hours across the state miserably bumping around while dodging myriad potholes. Smooth roads and functional bridges are not the reasons tourists vacation here, but they do play a large role in the overall experience and can even prompt some to not return. "The bigger issue is when your first impression and last impression of South Carolina is potholes and traffic jams, invariably some visitors will end up going elsewhere," Brad Dean, Myrtle Beach Area Chamber of Commerce president and CEO, told the Associated Press in January 2015. Trucking also comprises a sizable industry in the state and is entirely dependent on the interstate and highway systems. It is in all users' best interests to improve our freeways.

South Carolina's neglected transportation system became all the more obvious with the widespread flooding from Hurricane Joaquin. Even before the catastrophe, 1 in 9 bridges in the state were structurally deficient, equating to 1,031 bridges needing repair, according to Transportation for America. The raging waters demonstrated the state's problematic infrastructure to the country and to South Carolina's own citizens. The U.S. News website reported eleven dams toppled, and more than 300 bridges closed, further compounding the already ever-present issues. However, this attention can bring change.

With the flood came a silver lining: now may be just the right time to begin to ameliorate our problems. Citizens, more than ever, are sympathetic to the cause, and federal aid designed to help South Carolina recuperate from the flood is just the starting point. Now is the hour to pass legislation to raise the gas tax, which comprises ninety percent of the state highway fund, according to the SC Alliance to Fix Our Roads. The *State* newspaper reports that South Carolina's gas tax is set only at 16.75 cents per gallon and has not been raised since 1987, not even to keep up with inflation. Few would argue that an increase would hurt citizens; over time, money would be saved through decreased vehicle costs. The time is ripe to solicit support to raise the gas tax and reconstruct our infrastructure. Hurricane Joaquin drew scrutiny to our failing roads and bridges, but it also provided the groundwork for catapulting a solution into progress.

Raising the gas tax is a solution to repair South Carolina's decrepit roads and bridges that will benefit all. Users' cost will decrease as a result of fewer crashes and pothole problems; roads will be smoother for citizens, tourists, and truckers; and the safety of our bridges will improve. In April the House and Senate introduced plans to combat our failing infrastructure; all that is left to do is to compromise to pass a bill to make South Carolina a better place.

A World to Explore

Aimee McVey

A little girl wanders the elaborate streets of Saint-Malo, France, in her mind, blind and thoroughly alone. Her father, the master locksmith at the Museum of Natural History in Paris, was gone when the bomb hit, decimating her great-uncle's home where she lives. Marie-Laure is thinking about her father. Navigating the streets comes easily to her; her father loved building complex wooden models of her surroundings for her to explore with her fingers. His ingenuity inspired her life—all he did was for her. After Marie-Laure went blind at the young age of six, her father began saving up to buy her novels written in Braille, an almost unheard-of luxury in the pre–World War II era. She began to read, and read, and read the same books over and over again, consumed every waking minute by the adventures of Captain Nemo in *20,000 Leagues Under the Sea* by Jules Verne. Marie-Laure, one of the main characters in *All the Light We Cannot See* by Anthony Doerr, inspired me to share my love of reading and learning as a tutor for middle school children.

My first day I walked into the classroom terrified out of my mind. How would I, only a high school junior, be able to teach all that I know? How would I affect my student's learning? I wanted to do the best that I could, to benefit her to the best of my ability. Julia arrived and began chatting away instantly. I asked her how she was doing, and we soon began working on her math homework. She was far behind her fellow classmates; as a sixth grader, she still hadn't nailed down the essential multiplication tables. That first day I sent her home with a mission: learn those tables, and math will become so much easier.

Every week at lunchtime, I hastened down to the middle school to make some progress with Julia. Those tutoring sessions soon became my favorite part of the day. We would have so much fun solving problems together, and Julia's progress was easily noticeable. She mastered her multiplication tables and began to enjoy figuring out the geometry and pre-algebra problems. When she finished and showed me the correct answers with a proud grin, I couldn't help but smile. By the end of the year, she had raised her test grades from consistent Cs to triumphant As. We were both elated when she brought back that first A. I had succeeded in enveloping her in my love of learning, and she had accomplished goals that she hadn't thought she could. She had become my own Marie-Laure, full of excitement, venturing into the unknown and discovering joy in taking on the world. At the end of the year at the middle school awards ceremony, Julia was awarded the Most Improved Math Student for 2015. She had graduated from my teaching and was set to conquer the world on her own.

I enjoyed that first tutoring experience so much that I took on two more students in the next year. We journeyed through everything from long division and algebra to the rock cycle and *The Report Card,* a novel by Andrew Clements. I spread my love of learning, and my students taught me. They illustrated never giving up when a topic was difficult and taking on extra work in order to truly master a subject. They bounced back from bad test grades and celebrated when they achieved As. Though sometimes the work was difficult, they were able to fight through it and accomplish what they set out to do.

I have always been gifted at school subjects. I've always loved to read as well, so I could never comprehend the fact that some of my peers hated to pick up a book. Tutoring introduced me to kids who truly wanted to learn but soon were left behind in the dust as the class moved on before they had accomplished the new skill. I was able to walk in their shoes, bravely keeping their heads up over the flood of information. I truly could help them do what they had always wanted: learn about the world around them. Tutoring showed me that learning can be fascinating for everyone; you must simply engage the student in the process. As a leader and helper, I showed my love of searching and discovering, just as Marie-Laure does in all aspects of her life—exploring museums, walking through Paris, diving into her books, and ultimately maneuvering her way through World War II.

As Anthony Doerr's prose captivated me and drew me into discovering the lives of a young girl and boy during World War II, so do I hope to compel my students to be riveted by the world around them.

A Melody to a Nightingale

Kenni Ojediran

I was becoming Daniel in the lion's den. As I walked into the conference, ravenous gazes besieged me. I was bare. No armor of courage or ambition shielded me. No God there to save my tainted soul. The men straightened as I took my seat at the round table. Toothy smiles were creeping on their faces, and they collectively nodded in acknowledgement.

"Miss Amelia," one of the men said, stretching his paw toward me, "please begin."

I am fluent in two languages: the English language—common in several countries—and the language of song, spoken by the selected few who have effortlessly conquered its eternal melody and fluid scales.

I become another being when I sing. I am an ethereal entity when I fall into the familiar intervals and fortissimos. When I'm not singing, I am Amelia, the sixteenth alto in the choir. But when I sing, I have no name. I am another that had been dormant between teeth and tongue. I become the Nightingale, trapped in a vision and a waking dream.

High school caged me. Clipped my wings and twisted my ballad into cacophony. The program was rigid, and we couldn't afford the proper funding for our activities. We didn't even have an auditorium. No place for people to enter and hear our luminous hymns and sorrowful laments, invoking buried emotions and concealed tears. The prospective concert hall was replaced by a gym and hallways as winding and labyrinthine as they were before. Recognition was evident every time I gazed at those benches during concerts. I saw the familiar faces of the mothers, fathers, brothers, and sisters. There was no face I didn't recognize as I stood on those stands. I ached for a foreigner to stumble over the obscure language of song. They would watch me gracefully perform the routine and leave wanting to see us repeat our waltz.

"How do you expect we repair these problems, Miss Amelia?" A younger man was talking, bringing me back to the present. He smoothed back his mane as he stared at me from the edge of the table.

"Music is a form of expression for those who often can't express themselves in words," I explained. "But unlike any sport, physical exertion is not compatible with the arts. When I pursue my career, I may not want to be an athlete, a doctor, or an engineer. The art department should receive more recognition and more funding to encourage scholars to pursue what they love."

The council roared. Deep chuckles erupted from throats when I finished my plea.

"If this funding and recognition come to fruition, what do you foresee?" The man who had greeted me earlier grinned. But I was ready with my response.

"It would improve South Carolina by encouraging the artists and musicians," I told them. "The trumpet player, the soprano, and the violinist will be doing what they cherish. There will be more people who appreciate the arts in South Carolina, and more who will pursue arts-related careers. With this funding, our Nightingales will be freed."

Finding Expression

Kenni Ojediran

Her mind was a storm. She didn't speak, only her thoughts clouded over the pages, and my fingertips, flipping over them, were the thunder. This is a book called *Speak* by Laurie Halse Anderson. After being assaulted, Melinda Sordino, the main character, refused to speak. She internalized her agony and anger, unable to say what happened to her. But in the end she was able to express all the words she couldn't say. Each word was etched in her art.

Despite her silence, I understood her. I understood all the words she couldn't say; between every skirt she hated and drawing she threw away. I was like her: I didn't speak. I internalized all of my emotions, like Melinda had done, when my mother died. Each word would claw at my throat, searching for a breath to cling to. I felt enraged, confused, and afraid, but these emotions were too intimate. I was glass, and if I spoke I would shatter. I would be disrupted from my familiar arrangement and turned into a form that was sharper and hazardous. I couldn't express my feelings through a depiction of a tree. I couldn't convey every sentence in the branches, and each word in the leaves. But I was consumed by Melinda's story. In the end she chooses to speak. To save her friend from her assailant, Melinda was able to accept what happened to her.

By reading *Speak* I learned I could no longer hide my emotions behind teeth and tongue; I needed to find a voice. I needed to speak. I was finally able to acknowledge what had happened to me. Even if I couldn't express the words artistically, I was able to say it. I started to talk more at school, and I spoke to my family often. Each emotion that was so difficult for me to describe became easier to talk about, and each day without my mother became easier to live.

Finding the Answer

Morgan Rizer

The answer is education.

The answer is education because of the young hands of your cashier.

How they always have a perfectly balanced amount of nail polish chipped off and how they automatically wipe the thin layer of ice off your milk and how they artfully handle everything with care and intention, just like you imagine she handles everything in her life.

The answer is education because no one encouraged her, so her young hands will weather and age but will continue to attend to your groceries.

The answer is education because of the ways babies smell.

Their milky, powdery, delicate perfume always comforted you when you babysat neighbors' children in high school. That smell reminded you of possibilities and new beginnings. The young girl down the street felt that way too, until it was her own child wearing that perfume, and the new beginnings prevented her from finishing previous obligations.

The answer is education because she didn't think you could teach a child and learn yourself, so she stays at home and lets the comforting smell suffocate her. She will never have a new beginning.

The answer is education because of the whistle of your mailman.

His melodies are a mirrored reflection of his day. Sometimes, like on Tuesday after he ran into an old friend, they are nostalgic. Warm and brown on the edges and offering a small glance into the songs that carried him through high school.

The answer is education because those songs didn't get him past high school, so now he must pay for his worries by delivering families their own.

The answer is education because of the sweets in your favorite bakery.

They're so flawless and so decadent and make you feel as light as air. You once met the boy who makes them, and every day you smile at the perpetual streak of flour marking his brow. You also begin to notice that he keeps getting older and the store, less busy. You pause for a moment because you realize that he is too old to be here; he should be in a large university, using his hard-working hands to trace the intricate vines encompassing the school's old bricks. You mention this, and he shakes his head.

The answer is education because college is too far from home. He will continue making those heavenly sweets even after they become bitter on his tongue, because that is what he must do for his family.

The answer is education because of the eyes of your waitress.

How her best shift is the morning shift, just as the room fills with light. This is the time her green eyes, traced with a comforting gold, ignite you in the way her nineteen summers have enkindled her. Any cold left in your bones is eradicated quickly and forcefully, because it has no choice but to leave; snow cannot live if there is fire consuming it.

The answer is education because eventually those summers that warmed her will cause an inferno but then dissipate completely. Fires weren't meant to be contained, and if you don't give them room to breathe, they will die.

The answer is education because these hands and babies and whistles and sweets and eyes are the absolute essence of our people, and we must remind them that education is not an unattainable dream—that when you foster that innate desire to succeed beyond your limitations, you can do anything.

The answer is education because it is the foundation of our triumphs. Because of all the problems we face, South Carolina will find answers in education. We will find answers in painting higher education as something we can all have and something that will have a long-term effect on our lives. Showing our youth the necessity of education is the only shred of hope we have for advancement. Education is our key to the future.

The Craving

Morgan Rizer

Growing up in South Carolina has shaped me in many ways. I am no stranger to warm skin, and the fizzes of sea foam whisper to me like an old friend. I am at ease when the sun shines in its unabashed way, because the Great South is all I have ever cared to know. She has been kind to me and has raised me gently, and the only fault I can place on her is a lesson she taught me in my formative years. Through the sunset drives with music blasting, through my mama's homemade fried chicken, and through my neighbor's perpetually glowing tan, the South has taught me to crave.

This craving isn't just any old craving, let me tell you! The way I was raised taught me to always hunger for the feeling I got when my daddy and I would lie in our endless backyard at night and allow ourselves to be consumed by the silence of the stars and the humming of crickets. It's a feeling where being outside in the forest felt like home and where I knew I was completed once I was among the grass and birds and wind. I was taught to crave a relationship with nature and with the slow-paced, harmonious lifestyle it cultivated.

The need for this feeling grew within me every day and threatened to eat me whole recently, just as I began my senior year in high school. I blinked my eyes at the end of my junior year and found that I was a senior who had unknowingly succumbed to the Concrete Routine. I was always so busy with studying, with working, or with trying to figure out my future that I got lost somewhere and was stuck in this routine of going through the motions in order to earn a spot in the future I wanted. I was chasing my future and didn't even see that I was paying for it with my present.

So now this is the point in the story where I'm supposed to reveal the big, grandiose secret that got me to realize what went wrong—perhaps that I lost a friend or ran into a prophet or (heaven forbid) fell in love. But no, it wasn't like that. My great awakening came with a trip to Barnes and Noble, where

I found *I'll Give You the Sun* by Jandy Nelson. It seemed silly at first, and the vague cover sporting only a quote from the book seemed odd, but simply on a whim, I bought it. I began reading it that night, and I was thrown off even more because this strange book with no cover art or description, uncovered in a bargain bin at a bookstore, was changing the way I felt about writing with every minute word marked on its pages.

The author told of twins who were connected in a way that absolutely inspired me. She wrote, "Jude and I have been together since the very moment we existed," and the revolutionary suggestion that the intimacy level of twins reaches all the way back to the very moment they were conceived and included every little part of their lives after that sparked an inspiration in me that I hadn't felt since those nights in my backyard.

The book made me think of humans and their mortality differently. The way she compared the characters to each other and the nature surrounding them, brought out their similarities in such a unique way that I was often at a loss for words. This book—this random assortment of markings and paper and thoughts—took me on a journey that brought me back to my childhood and made me realize the life I was currently living was not what was meant for me. I am meant to walk barefoot through miles of forest and to repeatedly fall in love with the wonder of nature. To feel at home in the world apart from the mundane, routine-filled lives we force ourselves to live in. I am the kind of person who thrives from knowing I am immortal, for I live on in the flowers growing by my toes and the people walking by my side. This book just had to remind me.

The Time Has Come

Melis Tirhi

In June 2015 *Vice* magazine published an article titled "Smiling Faces, Terrible Racists." It began with the opening line, "Just about every time I'm in the Carolinas, something racist happens to me." Unfortunately this undesirable portrayal of South Carolina has been popularized across the nation, fueled by the widespread broadcast of discriminatory events such as that presented in the July 2015 RawStory.com article titled "KKK Rally in South Carolina Exposes the Ugly Underbelly of Racism in the US." Quite regrettably, yet undeniably, South Carolina has become known as a mecca of racism and the center of a crumbling education system.

Hidden under the shadow of its ignoble reputation is the state's remarkable landscape. South Carolina harbors 187 miles of general coastline and 2,876 miles of tidal shoreline, as reported by the National Oceanic and Atmospheric Administration (NOAA), twelve lakes covering more than 683 square miles, eight national wildlife refuges, Francis Marion National Forest, of 258,864 acres, and Sumter National Forest, of 370,442 acres. The state is indubitably a remarkable natural beauty.

However, a state is only as powerful as its inhabitants. "South Carolina Ranks no. 1 for deadly violence against Women" was the headline of a story published by the *State* newspaper on September 15, 2015. As a South Carolina resident and survivor of domestic violence, it would be fairly easy for me to dismiss this state as being home to no more than a variety of immoral persons, yet I have experienced firsthand the warm hearts of our residents.

Last June I lived in the College of Charleston dorms during an internship with the Medical University of South Carolina—dorms not far from the Emanuel African Methodist Episcopal Church in which nine members of the congregation fell victim to the brutal mass shooting by Dylann Roof. Just days later I found myself paying respects at the foot of the church, surrounded by a checkered crowd standing together in grief; no gender nor race divided them. A sight both warming and powerful, it was certainly not a scene that would be found in a wholly prejudiced state.

There is power in the people of South Carolina, as there always has been. Easily forgotten are the times when South Carolina was a pioneer in the nation. In 1698, the country's first publicly supported library was established in Charles Town. Charles Town also is where Henrietta de Beaulieu Dering Johnston, a female pastel artist and the earliest recorded female artist, lived from 1707 until her death in 1729. On February 18, 1735, the first opera, Colley Cibber's *Flora* (also known as *Hob in the Well*), was performed at the Courtroom in Charles Town. Not to be forgotten is the grit of residents today as they repair and rebuild homes and lands after the October 2015 historic rainfall that flooded many areas of the state. Their perseverance is not unlike the character shown by citizens after Hurricane Hugo in 1989, a disaster causing $6.5 billion in damage—most certainly not a small feat to overcome.

However, the spirit of our residents does not equate to the state of our infrastructure. It was only recently—July 10, 2015—that the Confederate flag was lowered from the state capitol. A step greeted with approval from the majority of the nation, it was a stride that began to elevate and highlight the value of South Carolina. South Carolina does in fact have value, but it is difficult to portray when there are still existing laws such as Article 17, Section 4, which states: "No person who denies the existence of a Supreme Being shall hold any office under this Constitution." Whereas at times situations of discrimination may be up for debate, here it becomes clear that the stereotype of discrimination within South Carolina has been embedded into our laws.

South Carolina can matter, but it will not until we elevate ourselves and broaden our minds as we have done quite minutely, thus far, with a regrettable amount of delay. Both our youth and the elders of this state must recognize the value of what we hold in both our people and our landscape, and our government must realize that progress will be far from fatal. South Carolina is the ultimate underdog, but it won't come out on top until we change direction. Terrifyingly and promisingly, the fate of South Carolina is in the people and our strides toward the future.

Vanishing the Past

Melis Tirhi

The underbelly of fear is our pasts. We haunt ourselves with memory—recurring images of time slipped between the cracks. Kevin Powers, author of *The Yellow Birds,* comprehends this idea more than most, setting forth a novel on the horrors of memory, bringing to surface the true nature of human existence—the beauty and inadequacy of our dispositions, and the loose ends that are our only resolutions.

In *The Yellow Birds,* Powers speaks of two soldiers confronting the horrors of Afghanistan. One survives and is left to confront PTSD. The events Powers describes in his work are greatly specific to a soldier—events the average person would not likely witness or experience. However, there is a certain quality of universal applicability within the text—an elusive attribute achieved by Powers's ability to bring forth the common foundations that underlie human existence. Without question, I cannot speak of what awful proceedings a person endures during deployment, but I do know about that imprisonment of the human mind, and I too know the face of PTSD.

In middle school my favorite poem was "Oranges" by Gary Soto, a work about the fragile beauty of love. I was enamored with the tenderness in which Soto presented the concept of the first sparks of love. It was tender, honest, and naive. When it came time for my very own first love in my second year of high school, it was anything but. "Love" came to be synonymous with arguments, a loss of freedom, and hand-shaped bruises. Even the most clever among us all fail to recognize the beginnings of something malicious. It began slowly, then erupted suddenly—like a natural disaster. Every facetious remark grew to be a sinister stab at my self-worth, every bump a shove, and "I love you" a stamp of control.

Time dissipates faster than we can understand it, but the mind is a device of perfect recollection. These memories became parasites, taking control of the center of my existence—the very core of every thought or work I ever produced. The poison of remembering ran into every corner of my life, becoming the driving force behind my ultimate state of numbness and detachment from a life that was mine. However, literature has great power—the power to ignite thought. And all things resolve themselves in thought.

Powers ends his novel with the ultimate demise of both characters—the death of one and the literal and mental imprisonment of the other. Most often books serve to inspire us to attain or emulate the actions of the characters, but it is not what Powers wrote but what he did *not* write that came to steer my life in a different direction. That's when I knew the choice I had to make—to take my life back from the grasp of my memories, to free myself from my mind.

What was done to me is irrevocable, fixed in time and thought. I've played it over and over in my mind's eye, becoming a knot in time I spent too much of my life trying to undo. But it was the love for who I am, what I stand for, and all I hope to do in my lifetime that kept me from allowing this abuse to take the grasp of my existence. Some things can't be undone, understood, or revoked in any way. Sometimes we must simply abandon the past to make way for new beginnings. Unlike the characters in Powers's novel, I did not allow this to be my end. The axis on which my life pivots is no longer this event, the thoughts I have not of these actions. This life is my own.

You'll Have to Watch Yourself

Taylor Widener

"Oh honey you can't go out like that
All the boys will notice you. And if you get any prettier, I'm just gonna have
    to put a bag on
your head
And lock you in the closet."
I am ten years old and the words roll off my Me-ma's tongue like it is natural
    to worry
About the safety of such a young girl
Because of how she is presenting herself.

"They tease you because they like you.
That's just how boys are raised. They don't know any better. You'll have to get
    used to it,
That's just how the cookie crumbles."
It is my first year of middle school and my teacher is stern but not about this.
She is frustrated with my complaints
And asks me to sit down.

"That costume is too sexy.
You're too young to look so sexy, you'll have to watch yourself tonight. You
    never know
What people will do on Halloween,"
My Me-ma says as she examines the Wednesday Addams costume I made.
I am just a young girl, dressed as a fictional young girl.
But all the adult fear has stripped away my fictional tenacity.

"This place is your home.
No matter where you go, you'll deal with the same things. You're never going
    to find a utopia.
South Carolina will win you back one day,"
My dad warns as I show him my college plans.
I know he's right, that this place isn't any worse than the next.
But all life's fear and the pain have been experienced here
I always hoped there was a place I could escape.

"Anna Karenina runs from her problems.
She could have avoided her own death by addressing her woes from the roots
Instead of running when the foundation began to crack,"
says my English teacher as we discuss our summer reading.
I suddenly see myself in the faithless protagonist.
I was trying to call my avoidance bravery,
But to truly be brave, I must stay and change what scared me before.

Lessons from Russian Aristocracy

Taylor Widener

Anna Karenina was a weight in my bag, snug against the small of my back, causing me nothing but frustration on my walk back from work. I had spent hours working my way through what I thought of as a literary brick. The summer air was almost as stifling as the clunky English translation of Tolstoy's original Russian words. As I walked into my apartment, the air conditioner changed my physical atmosphere, but the mental strife remained. Faced with a whole summer of frustration ahead of me, I took a nap.

I've always been one with big dreams, in every sense of the phrase. But this dream was given to me by the afternoon, so delicately yet with intensity, like the colors of the sunset streaming through my blinds and discoloring the floor. I could see myself, carefully poised to make my next move. I was alert with anticipation, but there was something about the scene I knew could only mean that the act I was anticipating would be as disappointing as everything that had already happened. Suddenly the dream turned from an image of me to one of Keira Knightley, all decked out in her period clothing, personifying Anna Karenina. Anna held the same expression that I had held just moments before, with the same air of doom. The room seemed to close in, and I could hear the sound of Anna's sobs grow more and more muffled as the air seemed to turn to a nearly solid fog. I saw her cross the room and hurriedly rush out of the door. When the door clicked back into place, the room cleared, and I knew that Anna would be dead soon.

I woke up from my nap in a panic. I couldn't make any connection between my life and my aristocratic nightmare, but I knew those images bothered me. I chose to tuck the book away on my shelf, hoping that out of sight would truly be out of mind.

Avoidance seemed to work, at least for a few months. The fall semester started, and as we discussed *Anna Karenina* in class, it seemed to me that any dark prophecies the novel was transferring into my subconscious had been put to an end, until our last lecture. "Anna Karenina ran from her problems; she never looked around herself for happiness and expected the next big thing to be her savior. She was a casualty of her own fears and avoidance." The words of my English teacher seemed to echo within me. I was transported back to a room with a crying Anna perched at the edge of her bed.

She had once had so much—a husband who loved her, a son to care for—but she had left it all behind for something new. Vronsky was her more exciting option, but once she had him she needed something better. I had finally made the connection.

I was living my life in tomorrow. I was in a different state, on a different coast, in a different world. I had no sense of self in the present, because everything I knew about myself had been learned from imagined details of my future. What I saw as a collection of harmless goals had become an army of reasons why I couldn't get attached to my reality. I had friends I refused to appreciate because I knew I'd be gone within a year. I had hobbies I couldn't spend time on because they didn't fit into a carefully calculated plan to get me to my next steps. If I was always trying to be someone else, I'd never have the focus to be me. I was on a fast track to being a casualty of my own ambition. Anna Karenina may not have had the hindsight to save herself, but she was able to show me exactly what I needed to see.

Finding Liberation

Sarah Williams-Shealy

When I was young, my hair was a long sliver of sunshine and my eyes were a vivid blue. I had a keen sense of observation and a good memory. No child should have to watch her mother's blood seep from her broken and bruised lips at the tender age of three. But I did. My father abused both of us. Fourteen years later I still remember the pain and how my wrist was a sickening blue on that last Christmas Eve. I woke up the following Christmas morning the same as my mother, bruised and battered. My father walked away without repercussion. For years numerous police officers did nothing at all. Except make empty promises that were as hollow as their hearts. The day my father finally left of his own accord was supposed to have been bittersweet salvation.

It was the beginning of a darker hell for me.

I was six years old when my mother lost her mind. The look in her eyes changed in an instant—like a rabid dog turning on its owner, foaming at the mouth. I remember the first time she hit me. She lost her sense of remorse.

Two years passed. I was eight years old and in the third grade. In that time the events that transpired were a gradual progression of everlasting torment. I asked her if she was a robot. What happened to my real mother? Who was this lifeless machine? She had once cared so much for me, and I had once known that she loved me. Now I had no idea who she was—this bundle of lifeless gears and circuit boards caring for me. With her electrical shocks.

I came home to her raging against the voices. She heard them, but I never did. And God forbid I tell her I couldn't hear or see what she did. My objections were black and blue against my skin and tearstained cheeks. I came to school, hair in knots, smelling like a puddle of urine, two broken legs in less than six weeks of each other. The Obvious. The teachers and other school officials saw, and they kept their silence. Of course, what mandated reporter would dare to interfere with the madwoman and her sad little girl?

There was a call that year. They brought her in for an evaluation. All the deputies, the doctors, the people who were supposed to care. They didn't want to deal with her, so they sent her back home. Declaring the woman who heard voices from lighting fixtures as "mentally stable."

And so she stayed all those years with me. The people who were supposed to care continued to ignore me with my tearstained cheeks and mentally unsound mother. Every doctor, every teacher, every police officer. And she left her marks of a mother's love. Smashed blueberries, imprinted on my skin. Cracks in my bones, like an old brick wall. And she left her words deep within my skin. "I hope you die." "Please, kill yourself. I'll get money from the life insurance." Seventy-eight scars up and down both my pale arms.

One day she said something to the wrong person. A letter of lies, sealed and signed in my name. The monster finally turned inward and consumed itself. High on insanity, up on a shelf. She had gone too far this time, sending that letter to the FBI. Making it sound like I'd written the crazy letter. But no one ever bothered to see the truth.

And so they came with a warrant for both of us. Shackled an innocent child in cold metal chains and Velcro. Treated me like an insane criminal, when my mother was the guilty one. Something they might have noticed had they paid attention even once for all of those years.

The social worker handed me over to a foster family. "You'll be safe now, you're out of there."

Oh, but the universe has a sadistic sense of humor.

It is worse than living with my mother.

The emotional and verbal abuse amplified. I told my social worker something wasn't right, that I did not want to stay where I was. She ignored me and closed my case files.

Ignored by a mandated reporter, once again.

Remaining a victim of abuse.

It's been five years now.

Five years more of torture, of tears. Of waking up without a will to live. Forty-two more scars on my pale skin from those who "love" me, just like my mother caused before.

Everyone ignored my situation.

The South Carolina Department of Social Services never saved me.

No one did.

So I'm saving *myself.*

I'm breaking free and *never* looking back.

Salvation

Sarah Williams-Shealy

I was in eighth grade when I first read the book that forever changed me as an individual and my view of literature. It was almost as if the universe knew the exact point in time when I would need those printed words on a smooth cream page the most. I had experienced a terrible day. It was bitterly cold outside, and I was crumbling apart like a stale sugar cookie. I got on the bus, and when I was finally seated, I took out the book and opened it to the first page.

The bus ride allowed me an hour and a half to consume the text. Thirty minutes into my reading, I thought, "Where was this book when I needed it before?" For the first time in my fourteen years, a novel had proven to me what no person ever could—I was not alone. The novel is *The Rules of Survival* by Nancy Werlin, and within the depths beneath its sky-blue cover I found salvation for myself.

That salvation came from knowing a person had taken the time to craft a story I needed to read more than any other. No one else in my life knew what it meant to have a schizophrenic, abusive mother—and the pain that comes with it—but this small rectangular figure did. Several hundred pages of printed text were the loving arms I never knew.

My eyes brimmed with tears as I closed the book that evening. Despite the odds, the main characters made it out of their home situation with a mentally ill and abusive mother. I thought, "Maybe I can make it out someday, too." Until I picked up that novel on that day on account of fate, it had never occurred to me what I could do.

I had always wanted to be a writer, but now I knew I could be like Nancy Werlin. I could write my own story to touch the lives of other children with mentally ill parents like me, so they would no longer feel alienated. I could find my own way to tell them, "You are not alone, and you can make your own path someday."

Because I read *The Rules of Survival,* I was inspired to give to others what Nancy Werlin gave to me. I have started my own novel targeted toward children who have suffered abuse because they have a mentally ill parent. Werlin's novel inspired me to want to make a difference and spread awareness about abuse and how mental disorders impact families. I want my book to end up in the hands of a young person whose life I can change by allowing them to read the words they need the most. I want to give someone else the sense of hope that Nancy Werlin gave to me.

CONTRIBUTORS

AMAIRANY AGUIRRE is a 2016 graduate of Saluda High School, where Kelly Minick was her English teacher. She is majoring in business at Lander University. Amairany is the daughter of Margarita and Armando Aguirre of Saluda.

JAMIE ALTMAN is a 2016 graduate of Heathwood Hall Episcopal School, where Elise Hagstette was his English literature and composition teacher. He is studying American Sign Language at Midlands Technical College and plans to be an ASL interpreter. He is the son of Denise and Jim Altman of Columbia.

BAILEY BABB is a 2017 graduate of James F. Byrnes High School, where Susanne Cash was her AP English language and composition teacher. She is studying English and communications at Winthrop University and plans to work in publishing. She is the daughter of Karen and Chip Babb of Moore.

MICHELLE BARTON is a 2016 graduate of St. James High School in Murrells Inlet, where Paul Solomon was her English teacher. She is majoring in psychology at Harding University in Arkansas and plans to be a psychiatrist. Her parents are LuAnn and Jim Barton of Myrtle Beach.

CANDACE BEEBE is a 2017 graduate of James F. Byrnes High School, where Susanne Cash was her AP English language and composition teacher. She is majoring in middle school education at Anderson University and plans to become an English and history middle school teacher. She is the daughter of Lisa and Dale Beebe of Wellford.

TAVASHIA BERRY is a 2016 graduate of Summerville High School, where Jennifer Plane was her English teacher. She is studying library and information science at the University of South Carolina, and considering careers as an archivist, children's librarian, and author. Her mother is Wykethia Berry of Ridgeville.

ISSAC BLACKWELL is a 2017 graduate of D. W. Daniel High School, where Sandy Hall, Todd Howard, and Dr. Robert Kendrick were his English teachers. He is studying business and computer science at the University of South Carolina and wants to work in marketing and as a freelance writer. He is the son of Shana and Terry Blackwell of Anderson.

MORGAN BLANKENBECKLOR is a 2017 graduate of Dreher High School in Columbia, where Lindsay Hiller was her English teacher. She is studying science at the University of South Carolina and would like to be a marine biologist and help endangered sea animals. She is the daughter of Kathy and Clark Blankenbecklor of Hopkins.

EMILY BROOKE is a 2017 graduate of James F. Byrnes High School, where Susanne Cash was her AP English and composition teacher. She is studying microbiology with a biomedicine concentration at Clemson University and plans to be a physician's assistant. She is the daughter of Amy and Robert Brooke of Duncan.

DE-JAH BURTON is a 2017 graduate of Strom Thurmond High School in Johnston. Her English teachers during her years at Saluda High were Jason Stansel, Christy Roberts, and Kelly Minick. She is studying nursing at Aiken Technical College. She is the daughter of Felicia Johnson and Johnny Key.

MALLORY CLAMP is a 2016 graduate of Northwestern High School, where Patti Tate was her English teacher. She is studying general engineering at Clemson University and plans to be an engineer. She is the daughter of Ann and Ronnie Clamp of Rock Hill.

ALYSSA CONNER is a 2017 graduate of Scholars Academy in Conway, where Morgan Sellers was her English teacher. She is studying creative writing and English in the Coastal Carolina University honors program and plans to be a television writer. She is the daughter of Joyce and Jim Conner of Myrtle Beach.

BRANDI CUNNINGHAM is a 2016 graduate of Saluda High School, where Kelly Minick was her English teacher. She is studying early childhood education at Newberry College and plans to teach kindergarten. She is the daughter of Angela and Tom Cunningham of Leesville.

CHRISTIAN EITEL is a 2016 graduate of James F. Byrnes High School, where Susanne Cash was his English teacher. He is majoring in operations research at the US Naval Academy and plans to enter the US Navy. He is the son of Richard and Jennifer Eitel of Moore.

ALEXIS ETHEREDGE is a 2016 graduate of Saluda High School, where Kelly Minick was her English teacher. She is majoring in nursing at USC Beaufort. After becoming a registered nurse, she plans to continue her education and become a traveling certified nurse midwife. She is the daughter of Candice and Alexander Etheredge of Batesburg.

NICOLAS FERNANDEZ is a 2016 graduate of Saluda High School, where Kelly Minick was his English teacher. After graduating from Joliet Junior College in Illinois, he plans to major in mathematics or one of the physical sciences at the University of Illinois at Chicago. His parents are Maria Rodriguez and Rafael Fernandez.

SARAH FINLEYSON is a 2017 graduate of James F. Byrnes High School, where Susanne Cash was her AP English and composition teacher. She is majoring in health science at Clemson University with plans to be a pediatrician. She is the daughter of Kim Ryan and David Finleyson of Duncan.

ERIN HACKNEY is a 2017 graduate of James F. Byrnes High School, where Susanne Cash was her AP English and composition teacher. She is studying psychology and music at the College of Charleston and plans to become a therapist. She is the daughter of Kristen and Greg Johnson of Wellford.

MAXWELL T. HALL is a 2016 graduate of South Carolina Connections Academy and has been homeschooled by his parents, Carol D. and Stephen R. Hall of Anderson. He is a nursing major at Anderson University and plans to become a medical doctor.

ANDREW HERBST is a 2016 graduate of Dutch Fork High School, where Julie Taylor and Katherine Mewborne were his Honors English teachers. He is double majoring in business and liberal studies at the University of Notre Dame. He is the son of Katherine and Christopher Herbst of Irmo.

ALEXANDRA HURD is a 2017 graduate of Westminster Schools of Augusta, where Whitney Diehl was her English teacher. She is majoring in exercise science on a full scholarship at the University of Alabama and plans to become a pediatric occupational therapist. She is the daughter of Jennifer and John Hurd of Aiken.

HALI HUTCHINSON is a 2017 graduate of Green Sea Floyds High School, where Kris Howell was her AP English teacher. She is studying health promotion on a full academic scholarship at Charleston Southern University and plans to be a health care administrator. She is the daughter of Craig and Pamela Hutchinson of Nichols.

JAYNAE JEFFERSON is a 2017 graduate of Dreher High School in Columbia, where Lindsey Hiller was her English teacher. She is studying biology at Tuskegee University and plans to join the US Navy. She is the daughter of Rose and Jermaine Jefferson of Hopkins.

MEGAN JENSEN is a 2016 graduate of James F. Byrnes High School, where Susanne Cash was her English teacher. She is studying English and secondary education at Winthrop University and plans to be a high school English teacher. Her parents are Deanne and Greg Jensen of Wellford.

ABBY JOHANSON is a 2016 graduate of James L. Mann High School in Greenville, where Toni Cato was her English teacher. She is a biology major, focusing on zoology, at Wofford College. The daughter of JoMarie and Bill Johanson of Simpsonville, Abby is planning a career in zoological wildlife rehabilitation and freelance writing.

MYA' JOHNSON-JONES is a 2017 graduate of Dreher High School, where Lindsey Hiller was her English teacher. She is studying business and culinary arts at Johnson and Wales University in Charlotte, North Carolina, and plans to own her own restaurant. She is the daughter of Shelly Johnson of Columbia.

ELIZA KAPELUCK is a 2017 graduate of First Baptist School in Charleston, where Melissa Clark was her English teacher. She is studying international relations and foreign language at the University of South Carolina and plans to work in the US Foreign Service. She is the daughter of Anne and DuBose Kapeluck of Charleston.

ALAINA KIFFER is a 2017 graduate of Crescent High School in Iva, where Alex Smith was her English teacher. She is studying music performance and chemistry in the Shreyer Honors College at Pennsylvania State University and plans to be a professional musician in a symphony orchestra or pit orchestra for Broadway musicals. She also plans to write. Her parents are Deborah and Lewis Kiffer of Starr.

MANOGNA KOLLURU is a 2017 graduate of Mauldin High School, where Melanie Rivers was her English teacher. She is studying computer science at Clemson University and plans to work as a programmer. She is the daughter of Venkata Kolluru of Greenville.

KATHERINE KRISTINIK is a 2016 graduate of Hammond School, where Michele Priester and John McCormack were her English teachers. She is studying neuroscience and Spanish at Furman University and plans to enter the medical field. Her parents are Melanie and Larry Kristinik of Columbia.

ALAN LANXTON is a 2017 graduate of James F. Byrnes High School, where Susanne Cash was his AP English and composition teacher. He is studying theater arts at Young Harris College in Georgia and plans to be an actor. He is the son of Laura and Todd Lanxton of Woodruff.

SYDNY LONG is a 2017 graduate of Nation Ford High School. Heather Spittle was her English teacher, and she collaborated with creative writing teacher Beth Swann for *Voices,* the school's literary magazine. Sydny is studying biology, neuroscience, and medicine at Duke University and plans to attend medical school. She wants to be a pediatrician in a city hospital. She is the daughter of Stephanie and Mike Long of Fort Mill.

JARED MACK is a 2016 graduate of Andrews High School, where Kathy Ferdon was his English teacher. He is majoring in journalism at Coastal Carolina University and plans to be a journalist and author. He is the son of Sabrina and Theron Mack.

MILNER MARTIN is a 2016 graduate of Provost Academy South Carolina, where Kristen Goforth was his English teacher. He is studying musical theater at Piedmont College in Georgia and plans to take over the Baillie Players, his father's theater company. He is the son of Dorothy and William Martin of Inman.

ISIS MCNEAL is a 2016 graduate of Timmonsville High School, where Charlene McKnight was her English teacher. After graduating from Florence-Darlington Technical College, Isis plans to serve in the military and then enroll in a four-year university. Her parents are Arnette Vonda Burno and Marvin Burno of Timmonsville.

AIMEE MCVEY is a 2016 graduate of Spartanburg Day School, where Bill Pell was her English teacher. She is studying biomedical engineering at Duke University and plans to be a biomedical engineer or physician. She is the daughter of Laura and Jim McVey of Duncan.

PATSY MEJIA-ROCHA is a 2017 graduate of Goose Creek High School, where Nick Geary was her creative writing teacher. She is studying criminal justice at Trident Technical College. She is the daughter of Aracely and Alex Mejia of Goose Creek.

BREANNA MURRIN is a 2017 graduate of Spring Valley High School in Columbia, where Frank Harrison was her English teacher. She is studying mechanical and aeronautical engineering at the US Military Academy in West Point, New York, and plans to be a NASA astronaut. She is the daughter of Christopher and Sosun Murrin.

KENNI OJEDIRAN is a 2016 graduate of Chapin High School, where Amy Carter was her English teacher. She is studying English at the College of Charleston and plans to become an editor. She is the daughter of Priscilla Pearson and Joe Ojediran.

HANNAH JANE PEARSON is a 2016 graduate of the South Carolina Governor's School for the Arts and Humanities, where Mamie Morgan, Scott Gould, and Alan Rossi were her teachers. She is a student at the Calhoun Honors College at Clemson University, majoring in American Sign Language and minoring in creative writing. She plans a career as a speech pathologist and writer. Her parents are Alison and John Pearson of Easley.

JOHN STERLING POOLE is a 2016 graduate of Spartanburg High School, where Dr. Edwin Epps and Jessica Burke Stevens were his English and creative writing teachers. He is majoring in secondary education in English and psychology at the College of Charleston, with plans to teach high school English. His parents are Mary Jane and Roger Poole.

MORGAN RIZER is a 2016 graduate of Bluffton High School, where Lisa Sumner was her English teacher. She is studying political science at the University of South Carolina and plans a career in politics and political journalism. Her parents are Bridget Duncan and Paul Rizer.

ZYRIA RODGERS is a 2017 graduate of Gaffney High School, where Kristie Camp was her English teacher. She is studying psychology and sociology at Yale University and plans to be a psychologist. She is the daughter of Tiffany Rodgers and Jeremy Sarratt.

JASMINE SHABAZZ is a 2016 graduate of Greenwood High School, where Faith Evans was her English teacher. She is double majoring in public health and biology with a minor in women's and gender studies at the College of Charleston. Jasmine has been selected for a social justice cohort at the College of Charleston, where she is a Ketner Emerging Leaders Scholar. She plans to become a pediatric oncologist, international HIV specialist, or an epidemiologist. She is the daughter of Ernestine and Muhammad Shabazz.

ANNA SHEPPARD is a 2016 graduate of the South Carolina Governor's School for the Arts and Humanities, where Scott Gould, Mamie Morgan, and Alan Rossi were her creative writing teachers. An anthropology student in the Honors College at the University of South Carolina, Anna is considering a career as a family lawyer. She is the daughter of Sallie and John Sheppard of Beaufort.

HAMPTON SLATE is a 2017 graduate of James F. Byrnes High School, where Susanne Cash was his AP English and composition teacher. An international business student in the Honors College at the University of South Carolina, Hampton wants to serve others through business. He is the son of Kelly and Bobby Slate of Moore.

MELIS TIRHI is a 2016 graduate of Hilton Head Preparatory School, where Katy Hudak was her English teacher, and a former student of the South Carolina Governor's School for Science and Mathematics, where Ike Coleman was her English teacher. She is studying bioengineering at Northeastern University in Boston and plans to enter neonatal-perinatal medicine. She is the daughter of Yucel Henderson of Bluffton.

TAYLOR WIDENER is a 2016 graduate of the South Carolina Governor's School for Science and Mathematics, where Ike Coleman was her English teacher. She is majoring in biology and minoring in environmental science at Furman University and plans to enter the medical field. Her parents are Angela and Jason Widener of Summerville.

SARAH WILLIAMS-SHEALY is a 2016 graduate of Saluda High School, where Mary Bates and Kelly Minick were her English teachers. She is double majoring in English and education at Lander University's Honors College and plans to be a high school English teacher. Her parents are Kathy Williams and Paul Shealy.

ERINTRUDE WRONA is a 2016 graduate of the South Carolina Governor's School for the Arts and Humanities, where Scott Gould, Mamie Morgan, and Alan Rossi were her creative writing teachers. She is studying biology/premed at Kenyon College and plans to become a general physician. Her parents are Stacy and Jeffrey Wrona of Fort Mill.

www.ingramcontent.com/pod-product-compliance
Lightning Source LLC
Chambersburg PA
CBHW020551020726
47494CB00006B/2025